A Monk's Reply
to Everyday Problems

Selection of Fifty Dharma Talks
from across the World

Published in South Korea by Jungto Publishing

51-7 Hyoryeongno Seocho Seoul, Korea/ Zip Code 06653 / +82 2 587 8991

4361 Aitcheson Rd. Beltsville, MD 20705 USA / +1 240 786 7528

www.pomnyun.com/email:jungtobook@gmail.com

Translated by Rei Yoon

Edited by Seung Suk Lee, Simone Halley and Jungto Volunteers

with help of Kerry Raleigh, Gyungja Choi, Blake Hollonds

Cover and Interior Design by Misung Kim

ISBN 979-11-87297-16-1 03220

A Monk's Reply to Everyday Problems

Selection of Fifty Dharma Talks
from across the World

Ven. Pomnyun Sunim

Translated by Rei Yoon

JUNGTO

Contents

Sad

Afraid

Angry

Desirous

Dissatisfied

Lost

Inquisitive

About Ven. Pomnyun Sunim

Ven. Pomnyun Sunim is the founder and the Head Monk of Jungto Society. He is a mindful Buddhist practitioner and a Dharma teacher. Actively engaged in social issues, he is also a messenger of peace, an activist against poverty and environmental pollution, and philosopher that voices critique of our current civilization.

In 1988, he vowed to live a Bodhisattva's life that is free from suffering and commits oneself to the wellbeing of others. He therefore established the Sangha, Jungto Society with the motto, "Open Mind, Good Friends, and Clean Earth."

Since 2008, he began offering Dharma Talks to people in Korea, which soon spread all over the world. His Dharma Talks tour in Korea named "Hope" from 2011 to 2014 became very popular where over 600,000 people met him in 436 locations.

In 2014, he visited 106 cities around the world in 115 days and delivered 115 talks to more than 20,000 Koreans living overseas. This book is a partial record of that Dharma Talks tour. His Dharma Talks are now available online, on the social media and in print. and in paper books.

Currently, in 2017, he held "Happiness" and "Reunification of the two Koreas" speaking engagements all over South Korea. Ven. Pomnyun Sunim's words of wisdom can be accessed through his books, social media, YouTube, TV, and radio. He has published more than 50 books since 1994, and many of his books were #1 bestsellers in South Korea. He has over 1 million followers in South Korea's most popular messaging platform KaKao Talk, 100,000 daily downloads of his podcasts, and over 300 million views of his YouTube videos.

His extensive humanitarian works include: helping North Korean refugees in the late 90s and efforts in trying to deliver aid to the victims of food crisis thereafter; providing education for the Untouchables of India since 1994; and building schools and developing communities for the marginalized people of the Philippines, Cambodia, Laos, Myanmar, and others.

In recognition of his humanitarian work, he received the Ramon Magsaysay Award for Peace and International Understanding in 2002 and the POSCO TJ Park Community Development and Philanthropy Prize in 2011. In 2015, Ven. Pomnyun Sunim received Kripasaran Award from the Bengal Association at the 150th Birth Anniversary Celebration of Ven. Mahasthavir Kripasaran, for his efforts in reviving Buddhism in India.

About the translator

Rei Yoon spreads Sarm Natural Farming across the world that tries to heal the soil, heal the people, and help the poor. He is a believer in individual awakening and follows the Buddhist teachings that can grow one's soul. He is a member of SARM Society (non-profit) and CEO of Soil and Soul Inc. A graduate of Seoul National University, he has formerly worked in the Foreign Ministry and Defense Ministry of Korea. He practices traditional Yang-style Tai Chi (Rainier).

Ven. Pomnyun Sunim's Dharma Talks

Ven. Pomnyun Sunim's Dharma Talks has no rules; people can ask, speak, and discuss any topics that they face in their lives. Issues range from the personal to societal, religious to scientific, civilization to nature. Ven. Pomnyun Sunim listens to people and guides them by the Dharma. He presents them a path that liberates them from sufferings. It is a conversation of liberation and happiness. Many people obstinately try to change "others" in the belief that that solves the problem. However, this rarely is the case and it is often neither possible nor desirable. The key is how "I" perceive things. Changing "my" own mindset opens the path to liberation.

The Talks will help you escape the grip of your own thought. Then you will be able to put yourself in the other person's shoes. Finally, you realize that dwelling in agony solves nothing. It might be suffering from one angle, but from another angle, it is not. Finally comes the realization that there is nothing to suffer about.

The teachings are a perfect replication of the Four Noble Truths of Buddhism — suffering, the cause of suffering, the cessation of suffering, the path to the cessation of suffering. It is not an invention of Ven. Pomnyun Sunim; it is what the Buddha has taught us with his life. Ven. Pomnyun Sunim does not need to explain the Four Noble Truths in themselves but in the course of answering the questions, the Four Noble Truths are naturally revealed. Talks make the questioner realize that there was nothing to suffer about. It awakens people's inner wisdom.

Ven. Pomnyun Sunim's messages are clear and unambiguous. There is no complicated or abstruse theory. He always talks of enlightenment and practice on a level-ground with the questioner. Through his words, you will understand how practical Buddhism is, how close it is to our everyday lives. Awaken your inner wisdom, for that is the Diamond that breaks through ignorance.

Preface

For 115 days, from August to December of 2014, I traveled 106 cities in over 50 countries across the world to offer Dharma Talks. I met people, real-life people in their real-life situations. I listened to their questions and shared their issues of life ranging from light-hearted curiosities to dead-serious issues. My long travel took me across both Americas, Europe, Australia, New Zealand, and many parts of Asia. It taught me one thing: the problems that bother us are not much different. Indeed, they are universal questions. For we are all the same in that we are part of the humanity.

I tried to answer them as best as I could, not from my personal standpoint, but from the perspective of Buddhism. Contrary to common belief, Buddhism is an extremely practical religion, full of simple to profound wisdom that can immediately and directly be applied to our lives. The insight taught by the Buddha more than 25 centuries ago remains a treasure chest, waiting to be opened by modern-day people. We have only to re-discover what was delivered to humanity by the Great Saint that had come to us at the dawn of civilization.

The particular conditions that make up a person's life significantly influence the quality of happiness they feel. That is why people are on an endless journey to change their conditions. However, liberation lies in forgoing these conditions. I probably answered questions from over a thousand people during the 115 Dharma Talks. Some were rich, some poor, some young, some old, some married, some alone, some successful, some failing. All in all, few were happy. Yet they all tried to change their conditions, from one condition to another.

I want to ask you a question, the fundamental question of Buddhism, "Why do we suffer?"

Pause for a moment and think. Why do you suffer? What can stop the suffering? Is your action the right response? Are you on the path to happiness?

We cling to questions in life that we have created. We suffer from the sufferings that we believe exists. We do not realize that they are there because we see them as being there. Indeed, we have constructed them where they are constructed. They are solid and real only as much as we believe them to be.

We should all be happy, and happy always. All beings deserve to be happy. There is no reason to suffer. Being alive itself is a blessing. Whatever the experience, whatever the circumstance, whatever the challenge, you have the right to be happy, you can be happy. Happiness is not something you pursue, because happiness is right here. It always has been. There can be no precondition to happiness. Happiness is not a result of conditions but rather a state of surpassing all conditions. That you are able to see, hear, and eat are all blessings. Do not "try" to be happy. There is nothing to try for. You should be happy now, not tomorrow, not next week, not when you have achieved success. There is no path to happiness; there is only the path of happiness. Happiness is where you stand.

How can you be happy? You have to be awake, to be aware, whether you are a Buddhist, a Christian, or have no religion. You should practice. The Buddha and Jesus both maintained the attitude of happiness to the very moment of their deaths. What we should follow is their attitude toward life, not the specific religious establishment or doctrines created by later followers. This walking the path of happiness is called "practice." You can choose to prostrate, pray, meditate, volunteer, donate, or whatever. Whatever the path, it should make you happy. Now and tomorrow, here and end, you and I should be happy. That is sustainable. True happiness is not temporary.

Look at things with positivity. Whatever it is that has happened, look at it from a positive viewpoint. However, a deeply hardwired negative perspective is very difficult to change. This is called karma.

This book contains fifty conversations selected from a Korean book published in 2015 after my 115-day Dharma Talk tour across the world, in front of various audiences. They were carefully reviewed and translated for English-speaking readers. This is the fruit of such efforts.

Start living a happy life right here, right now; that is the beginning of change.

Fall of 2018
Pomnyun

Sad

Is it not wonderful that things have no meaning?

Why be sad about things being meaningless?

Wouldn't it be sadder if things indeed did have meaning?

I miss my deceased son

/

Tokyo

/

A lady asked, "It's been thirty-two years since I came to Japan. I had a son who suddenly passed away last year. I didn't even know he died. I found his body two days after his death. When I opened the door to his house, he was dead. He had died from overworking. He was such a nice boy. He never gave me any trouble. I was just utterly lost. I did a traditional 49-days funeral for him. Now I take sleeping pills and abuse alcohol. My husband is sixteen years older than me. My only concern is that I should live as long as he lives. But in my entire mind, I am only thinking of how to die."

Do you believe in a soul that lives after death?

"Sometimes I feel it exists and sometimes I don't."

Say your son's soul is here with us. If he sees you in such suffering, would he be happy or sad?

"He would be unhappy."

Why are you doing something that your son would dislike? What you are doing is exactly what your son would have feared the most. One more thing. People say Heaven is better than this world. Your son has gone to a good place. What is there to be sad about? He is in a wonderful place. Yes, you miss him but still, he is in a beautiful place now.

Let me ask you, would you have wanted him to get married? Would getting married have been good for him?

"Yes."

If he had been married, he would have left you anyway. Separation would have come nevertheless. It is understandable that you feel sorry for the loss. But think differently. If your friend is demoted and assigned to a bad position, that is regrettable. But if your friend was promoted and is working in a better position, that is good. Your son is in a wonderful place. Do not anguish.

I fully understand that you are grieving. You lost a son whom you brought into this world and have raised with love. He is in a good place now. Do not worry. The problem is that what you are doing is exactly what your son would have worried about the most. What should you do not to make your son worried? Should you continue to weep and grieve? Or should you recover and live happily? Be happy for your child's sake. Let

Good-bye! Sayonara! Let go from the heart.

Let go of the attachment.

That is called delivery.

Your son cannot be delivered if you hold on.

Just release and live happily.

him rest. You are a mother. Why do you make your son suffer? Imagine your son is looking down at you from Heaven. Please comfort him. From today on, let him say, "It hurt me so much to watch my mother suffer. But I am truly relieved that after meeting that monk that day, my mother has come back to being normal and lives happily."

What does your death do to help your son? When you are alive, do not try to die. When you are to die, then die well. Got it? Trying to die and trying not to die are both not good. Just live happily and die well when the time comes. Don't be too sad. Do you go to church or temple?

"I used to be a Catholic. But since my son's death, I've been afraid to open the doors of the cathedral. I feel like there is no God. My sister took me to a Korean temple. I studied Buddhism with a monk for one year."

In Christian words, you should say, "Thank you, Lord." Why? Because he took your son to Heaven. It is a wonderful thing.

"I cannot say that. The door to my heart is shut."

You are not a genuine Catholic. Open the door again, go to God and pray, "Lord, let your will be done. Thank you for taking my son to your side." Life and death are arranged by the Almighty alone; you have but to accept. In Buddhism, we say that your son's karma was such. His life here was to finish in such a way. Just tell him, "I know you had a hard life here.

Now you don't have to be like that in Heaven. Continue to live happily. I will live happily on my part. When the time comes, I will join you."

It is okay to switch between church, cathedral or temple. Do you think God would be upset? Well, in my view, God is more generous than that. Go wherever you can find the greatest consolation. In Catholic terms, you should not have any complaints about the doings and workings of God. It is all the Lord's will. Just thank him. In Buddhist terms, just say, "Your life here was planned only for such. I hope you will be born again in a wonderful place. I hope you do not need to overwork in your next life." This is how you should do it. Got it? Now, will you cry or not? Are you going to change your mindset and live happily or not?

"I was getting ready to die… I had to get things organized. What of my property, of my house…"

How can someone planning to die worry about the house? You will never kill yourself. (Laughter.) If you want my help, give me your house. I will take care of it. (Laughter.) Please. Do not think of death. Live with joy. Your only way to meet your son is to live well. You see, your son is in Heaven but if you commit a suicide, you will go to Hell. Then you cannot reunite with him. I am talking under the assumption that souls exist. However, I am of the position that whether or not souls exist is of no relevance. It does not matter whether they exist or not. It is not important whether Heaven exists or not. What is important is that you live a life that deserves going to Heaven. How you go to Heaven is described in the Holy Bible, in the Buddhist canon, and more. That you live such a life is important. If your present life is happy, your next life can also be happy. If you are unhappy today, you will be unhappy tomorrow. If you live your life in recklessness like now, your next life will be the same. That is why you have to eradicate all bad karma while in this life.

If you keep calling your son, he cannot enter Heaven. If you keep holding him, it will hamper him from moving on. He will become a lonely lost soul. That is the worst thing that can happen to a spirit. You are making him just that. Let him go. Let him move on. So that he may enter Heaven or paradise or whatever. Is it better to hold him or to let go?

"It is better to let him go."

Then repeat after me. Say, "Good-bye, my son!"

"Good-bye, my..."

No. No. Don't cry like that. Crying means you don't want him to go. You are trying to fool me. But I am not easily fooled. It must come from the bottom of your heart. Shout out, "Good-bye, my son!" You have to speak with sincerity.

"I was happy because of you. I miss you so much. I heard Ven. Pomnyun

Sunim's teachings today. I will try my best to let you go from my heart..."

No. No. That is too long. Also, don't "try" to do something. If you are trying to let him go, that also means you do not want to let go. That is called an "effort." We don't like efforts. Keep it brief. Just say, "Good-bye, my son!"

"Good-bye, my son! Sayonara!"

Yes! Well done! Just let go. Live happily. That is a good life. God will like it. The Buddha will approve it. Why do we do a 49-days memorial service? It is a journey of letting go of your loved ones. It is a ritual to let go of the attachment. Funerals and rituals are of no use if you still have that tight grip inside you. It is ultimately about your heart. If your heart lets go, the ritual has been perfected.

I am lonely

An elderly lady explained, "In my 20s and 30s, I was too busy working and raising kids; I had no time to feel lonely. Now, that my kids have all grown up and I have a lot of time, I am sometimes lonely. I have my family, friends, and brothers and sisters; yet, I feel alone. Share with me your wisdom for this."

We say that modern people are lonely in the crowd. Why is it that you are with so many people yet feel lonely? Why is it that you see your husband every day, yet you are lonely? You are with others but are not with them. Your heart is shut; that is why you are lonely. Even if you live by yourself in the mountains, if you have an open heart, you are not lonely. You can talk to the trees, birds, and feel as joyful as ever.

If you shut your heart, even if you live and sleep with your husband, you will still be lonely. It is not your spouse's fault. It is that your mind is shut.

Imagine if you were very busy. If you had urgent work that you must finish, you'd have no time to feel lonely. This loneliness is arising from within you because, up to now, it had been suppressed. Suppressed because you were busy. But now that you are at ease, these feelings are surfacing. It is like meditation. When you start meditation, all sorts of suppressed ideas and desires will be unleashed.

Observe yourself. Use this opportunity to realize your state of mind. Realize that your heart is tightly closed. Forgetting loneliness by making yourself busy is not the solution. Try to reach a state where you have a lot of time, are at ease, in meditation, but throughout the whole day, you are nothing short of happy. Most important is that you realize, "It is because of my karma that I am lonely. I see that I am not opening my heart."

You look as if you are too much imprisoned in your own thoughts. Relax a bit and start talking with your husband and kids. Why would you shut yourself in? This kind of inclination is formed at youth. Most parts of our psychological tendencies are decided when we are very little. Children are likely to copy their mothers. Or children have certain experiences that form the basis of their subconscious. This subconscious will be active, like a player hidden behind the curtain, for the rest of their lives. Understanding this is critical. Only then can you know you.

You must realize that loneliness has arisen in you not because you came to Norway, not because of some fault of your husband, but because of your own karma. Loneliness is shaped by how your karma is shaped. The problem becomes how to overcome karma through practice. Keep telling yourself, "I am comfortable." If you keep doing this, a conflict between the autosuggestion and the uncomfortable reality will arise. Keep doing it. Keep telling yourself, "Thank you for everything. I am so comfortable." Then, a moment will come when you realize the cause of your discomfort.

The goal of our conversation is to make your heart a little bit lighter. Enlightenment is about letting go of your view. Your perspective has been stuck to just one angle. By releasing it, you can see the object from all angles, from the side, up and down. Then you realize that what you held onto tightly as a problem is a problem no more.

Being able to see the whole picture is called insight. This insight is wisdom. People wonder, "How does enlightenment eliminate suffering?" You see, if you have the insight, many of the defilements will melt away. Turn on the light, and darkness will retreat. Darkness does not need to be removed; it simply vanishes.

What is important is not the type of faith you have but the way in which you perceive the operation of your mind. Perceive positively and you will be happier. Perceive negatively and there are abundant reasons for grief. High expectations give back high dissatisfaction. Low expectations return low dissatisfaction. The perspective that I choose determines the happiness that I enjoy. This is not all. But make it a starting point.

Oslo Domkirke

My friends have betrayed me

Oakland

A middle-aged man asked, "It has been thirty years since I came to the States. I had three very close friends. I have never once had any doubt about our friendship. Eight years ago, I suddenly lost my family member. I wanted to share my grief with my friends. But I was completely shocked when none of them came to the funeral. They were not there at the time of my greatest need. If I had done something wrong, I could understand, but there was no such thing. The sense of betrayal and anger was overwhelming. They never explained.

Recently they started contacting me again. I firmly told them that I do not wish to see them. One part of me actually wants to forgive them and have a good time like before, but whenever I think back to that horrible period, I cannot open my heart to them. What should I do?"

I understand that you may be hurt. But let me point out that it is actually you who didn't treat them as true friends. If you trusted them as a true friend, instead of thinking, "How can they do this to me?" you would have thought, "There must have been some circumstances I am not aware of."

Let me tell you a story. Once there were two very close friends. One person was sentenced to death by the authority due to some misunderstanding. This person said, "If I have to die, I will accept that. But I have an old mother. Please let me go to her to say good-bye. I will come back, and then you can execute me." The prison guard said, "How can I trust that you will return?" His request was denied. So this person asked his friend. The friend eagerly said, "I will stay in prison for you. Go see your mother." The prisoner was freed under the condition that if he did not return, his friend would be executed. Guess what? The prisoner did not return on the promised date. The prison guard taunted the friend, "You are a fool. Did you really think that the guy would return? He certainly ran away. I have no choice but to kill you." He was getting ready to hang the friend. The man said, "My friend is not a backstabber. There must have been some circumstances. Please tell him not to be too sad after I die." It turned out that the prisoner, while on his way back, was badly beaten by some robbers and fell unconscious for days.

What do you think? Listening to your story, it seems that to you, your friends suddenly cease to be friends if they don't contact you when you are in need. Do you think you yourself are a true friend to them when you have refused to see them after eight years? You grip on to the thought that you were betrayed, that you are the victim. But your friends might have something else to say.

You need to make a choice. "Those terrible people never were my friends. I wanted them to help me when I needed them but they did not. That is not what friends are for." Is friendship is a give-and-take? You are making friends so that you can benefit. This is not different from a business. And when they cost more than they benefit for you, you cease to do business with them. It is the same as a shop going out of business. Close the "Friends" shop.

However, if you can change your views and think, "I see that it was I who did not treat them as true friends. I was too gripped by my own thoughts," you might want to meet with them. At the very least, should you not meet with them and listen to what they have to say? They might have some unexpected answer. For example, they could have been in as much of a panic as you were at the time of the tragedy or they could have chosen to leave you alone for a while or whatever. Then you might end up saying, "I see that that was why. I was hurt because you did not give me what I wanted. But now I understand. I am sorry." This can be a way out.

The man replied, "Listening to your words, I think that maybe I should at least have had some conversation with them. But what I cannot understand is that there were a total of three friends, not just one. How could they all choose not to contact me?"

Is that really so difficult for you to understand? With the experience in life that you've had, this cannot be a particularly difficult thing to accept.

One person in the audience commented, "Your answer is too idealistic. We can't use that in our day-to-day lives."

Let me answer that. Assume I replied, "I think those three friends of yours are worthless. Do not bother being friends with them. Never see them again." Is that more realistic? The audience might be thrilled but this answer does not help the questioner. The gentleman that asked the question, a part of him wants to have his friends back. If he had no lingering feelings toward his friends, he never would have asked. Of course, the feelings are mixed. Another part of him wants to abandon his friends and not look back. Eight years have passed, so he is able to ask. I suspect the two parts of his mind are fifty-fifty. That means even if he didn't ask me today, if another three years go by, he is likely to contact his friends. That is because negative emotions weaken with age. Was my reply realistic?

The man replied in tears, "Definitely. It helped me a great deal. I will go back and get in touch with my friends again. Thank you very much."

I have deeply hurt my mother

/

Istanbul

/

A young lady asked, "I have lived my life as I wanted. It has been perfect other than one thing that I regret. When my mother was running her business, I had a disagreement with her and had told her, 'I will never see you again.' And now that time has passed, I want to heal my mom's trauma but how should I do that?"

To me, it looks like it is your problem and not your mother's. You have trauma in you; that is the problem. Why do you say your mother is the one with the trauma? You are trying to be perfect. You are not able to forgive yourself for not being perfect. You want to erase your trauma because that, to you, feels like a big dirty spot that makes your life very much imperfect. This has nothing to do with your mother.

First, you have to accept that you are a human being with many, many flaws. You are not perfect. You are not errorless. The perceptions that religion cannot make any errors, that religious leaders cannot be wrong, that the communist party is the absolute good, etc. are a source of great evil in this world. We are all imperfect, and we have to accept ourselves as such. You are especially imperfect. You are imperfect to the extent that you are ready to say, "I will never see my mother again," if your mother is not to your liking.

Try to accept that you are imperfect. If this characteristic persists in you, when something in your marriage does not work out, you are very likely to tell your husband, "I cannot live with you." Your type, you see, is the one who tells kids, "I've had enough. I will never see you again." If you worked in a company where there was some dissatisfaction, you would instantly resign. "I am quitting and I am never looking back!" You have said unkind words to your mother; to whom would you hesitate to speak of in meaner words?

Realize that you are not perfect. That is not embarrassing. The world, you see, knows your imperfection. What a joke that you alone do not know this. Be wise; realize your imperfection before others do, more thoroughly than others can. Even when people praise you, tell yourself, "No, I have serious imperfections." You paid the price through a bitter experience. Do not waste that; learn. You have seriously hurt your mother; make sure that she is the last person you give pain.

Actually, you are lucky that you hurt your mother and not anyone else. If you had traumatized a stranger, that could have been a tougher situation. Make this an opportunity for change. Think to yourself, "I see that I am imperfect. I should be more careful when anger arises. When I get mad, I will breathe deeply and think once more. I will not jump to radical conclusions."

Go and bow to your mother and say, "Thank you, Mother. I've learned a lot from this experience." That will heal you. This has nothing to do with your mother. You are the one who is struggling with a painful memory. You are the one who is hurt, unable to accept the fact that your myth of perfection has been breached. If your clothes are white, a drop of ink will stand out. If your clothes are black, even a splash of ink will be unidentifiable. Do not try to be white, for you are not. Accept the imperfection.

You said, "I've lived as I wanted." That tells a lot about your personality. You look quiet but you have an adamant character. People with that kind of personality should especially realize the imperfection within themselves.

Your mother gave you the opportunity to realize that, so be grateful to her. I am not saying your mom was necessarily right at that time. Nor am I saying that what you said was wrong either. I am merely pointing out that because of that experience, you discovered the radical inclination within you, your karma.

Go to your mom, apologize for the harsh words you have spoken and ask her for forgiveness. If your mother forgives you, tell her, "Mother, I was young at that time and tended to speak with extreme words. Now I have learned that propensity within me and I am being more careful. Thank you for allowing me to learn."

Your mother might admit to her pain and say, "Yes, daughter, your words seriously hurt me." Then what do you say? "Forgive me, Mother. But that experience has made me wiser." That is better than saying, "I did wrong, I have been bad. It is my fault." If you are too apologetic, that might actually make your mother uncomfortable. You see, your mother has to open her heart, open her mouth, bring out and speak what she has kept deep inside for so long. That is her healing. Saying that she is okay does not mean that she is really okay.

Another possibility is that you bring up this issue but your mother might not even remember. She might just say, "Oh, yes, you said that. But I forgot all about it." Then you know that your cruel words did not hurt your mother.

However, do talk with your mother if that incident has been hurtful for her. If you tell her that you are sorry and that that experience actually made you grow mature, then your mother will likely be okay. That is how the love of a mother works. Seeing that her daughter is fine makes her feel fine as well. You will understand this once you have children.

So stop worrying about your mother's trauma. If you said that to your child, then that is different. You cannot do that to your child whom you have brought into this world, whom you have to be responsible for. Do not worry so much about your mother. I see that the pain lies in you, not in your mother. You have to heal yourself first to heal anybody. That is not being selfish. That is how it is. Only when I am healed, fulfilled and well, can I extend out to others to embrace their suffering.

This is not about your mother; this is about you.

Saint Mary Draperis Catholic Cathedral

Whether you believe in christianity or Buddhism,

whether you live in America or Korea,

whether you are a man or woman,

these are not important.

You can be happy in any situation.

I cannot accept
the deaths of my family members

/

Dallas

/

A lady asked, "My grandfather and cousin died a few years ago. Time has passed and I can accept that fact. But still my mind is not at peace. How can I become peaceful?"

When did the two pass away?

The woman replied, "Grandfather died at the age of seventy-one when I was twenty-three. My cousin died at the age of twenty-three, two years before that."

What happened?

"My cousin died from a traffic accident, and my grandfather from a heart attack. Both incidents were completely unexpected. I never had a chance to say good-bye. My heart would not heal."

I understand. There are few things in the world that match the shock of an unprepared separation, an unexpected departure, an unforeseen good-bye. If your parents die, that can be less of a shock, because all children would expect their parents to leave one day. However, if a child leaves before the parents, that pain is utterly, utterly unimaginable. So is the saying that, "When a child dies, you bury them in the parents' heart, not in the soil."

The deaths you referred to are different but still nevertheless traumatizing. They were both unexpected. Say you fought with your lover and decided to end the relationship. That is nowhere near as traumatizing as your lover suddenly vanishing into thin air overnight. When your mind is not ready, it takes much longer to heal. However, this is a matter of your own trauma. It is no longer the matter of your loved ones' deaths. Now it is your own problem. You must heal your soul.

The woman continued, "After those incidents, I am seized by the thought of death. I am worried about the deaths of my parents, my friends, everything."

There is a difference between experience and trauma. They are all events in life but experience strengthens whereas trauma destroys you. If you have experienced the deaths of your loved ones, you should be less shocked by deaths after that. You should be stronger when your parents pass away, you should even be able to withstand the death of your husband.

But once you are traumatized, the experience of further deaths does not make you stronger or ready for the future. Any future death will give you greater trauma.

When people fail in a relationship, some people overcome the failure, find another lover and manage the next relationship more maturely. Some people never overcome the first failure and refuse to enter any future relationships. Whatever it is that you go through, make it an experience, not a trauma. Experience is an asset, trauma a liability. In your mind is a deeply rooted fear, a fear that grew out of your shock after the first deaths you experienced.

Men and women can have a sexual relationship. When based on both people's love and consent, we call it love. When based on coercion and violence, we call it rape. Love is not a trauma but rape is completely devastating. Not only for the body, but the mind will bear an irreparable damage. These memories of sexual assaults stretch deep into the person's life. When a woman with a trauma meets a boyfriend or gets married, and the man makes a sexual expression, it may remind her of the trauma. This can jeopardize the entire relationship.

Something happened in your life that you neither expected nor wanted. Your thoughts have stayed in that moment ever since, frozen, seized by the thought of death. But a person can die anytime anywhere. Your parents could die tomorrow or even today. Who knows? But do not be afraid because you do not know. Remind yourself that you are more experienced and well prepared for those tragic events. Be positive. Nothing is eternal.

Relationships that we have entered are transient. Be good to your parents. Do not be traumatized even if they suddenly pass away tomorrow. Turn your trauma into experience. Do not think, "What shall I do if my parents die?" Rather think, "I fully understand that my relationship with my parents will come to an end someday. I will do my best for them today."

But your trauma was so intense at a young age that it is extremely tough to heal. There are many North Korean refugees who live in South Korea. They find it hard to adapt to a new society. It is not so much because the society is radically different, but rather because every time they see food, it reminds them of their families and friends who died of starvation. They need psychological therapy but when they escape to South Korea, our government focuses only on material assistance. Then often, they cannot get a job, end up using up the money they have received, and we fail to embrace them into the society.

You must heal yourself first. Try going to a counsellor. Open yourself and bring out all the things you have kept in you. Talking with me also helps. Your conscious accepts the reality but your subconscious resists. It would not accept the deaths. Death in itself is not something to be sad or afraid of, but it was the suddenness that left you traumatized. Now you have fear. You have to heal the mind; your mind is stuck to that incident.

Death and life always go together. I can die today; my father can die tomorrow. Do not be afraid. Conversely, use this fact to realize how precious your life is. Tell yourself that you will make the most out of every day. Every morning when you wake up, if you are a Christian, say, "Thank you,

Lord. Today is another day in your blessing." Give prayers of thankfulness. If you are a Buddhist, say, "Thank you, Buddha. Your blessing leads me to another happy day." If you have no religion, say, "Wow, I live again today! Thank you!" That is how you should pray. This is not a prayer in a religious sense; it is a healing.

Do not worry about the uncertainty of tomorrow. Instead, be grateful for the life you have today. Continue such prayer, and it can heal you.

I want to have a baby

A female student asked, "I am a student of Kyoto University. I am Korean-Chinese, have been married for nine years, but do not have a child. When people look at my husband and me, actually, there are lots of things for them to envy; both our parents are healthy, our sisters and brothers are well, we had a wonderful childhood. Our only problem is that we still do not have a child yet. What should I do?"

Did you see a doctor?

"Yes, we have been both examined. But the doctors say that neither of us has any health problem."

Have you tried in vitro fertilization?

"Yes, we have. We received assistance from doctors and did everything we could. However, we failed in everything we tried. It is not easy."

Conception is nature's work. You can get pregnant after being raped once. You can fail to conceive after ten years of marriage. This is nature's doing. There is no need to be obsessed.

There is an upside to being childless. You are working on your Ph.D.; it is easier to study without a child. Why must you have a baby? Are you not too stuck with old values? In traditional Korean societies, women were treated like baby-producing tools. Sometimes, the husband's family expelled the woman for failing to produce a son. But we are not living in such an era. Women can have their jobs, do work, live their individual lives. Why do you want a baby so much?

Another choice is to adopt a child. There are many, many abandoned babies; why must you make your own? Adopt one of those babies. You have grown up in China with Chinese traditional values and maybe that is why you think as such. If you really want a biologically your baby, try IVF.

"Maybe it is my fault. I have considered all three choices you just explained: IVF, not having a baby, and adoption. But I still feel ever so uncomfortable. I find it difficult to discuss this with my husband."

Why is infertility your fault? Doctors said your body is normal. You have no problem with your health. Why do you blame yourself for infertility? That is an obsolete way of thinking and it is wrong. What did you do wrong? Nothing. Why do you have to feel bad toward your husband or parents-in-law? You are a modern woman, studying for a Ph.D. at a university. You should get rid of those thoughts.

"My husband and I are both healthy. That is why it is all the more frustrating for us. If we knew the problem, we would address it. If we had a disease, we could treat it. But modern medicine has verified that we both have no abnormalities. Maybe it is the environment or stress factor, I don't know. I don't know how to deal with this."

If your body is normal but you do not have a baby, that means it is not time for you to have a baby. If you force your desire upon your fate, you might get into a trouble. What if you had a baby with a disability? Would you still be happy?

"I have never thought of that."

That is ignorance. Say you have a baby with birth defects, would you still be grateful and lovingly raise the child? Or would you rather not have such a baby? If you are the latter, your craving for a baby could be inviting a tragedy. You are not looking into how things are; you are preoccupied with your wish to have a baby. You need to relax.

It could be that not having a child at all could actually be good for you. That might be the fortune given to you. Look how many parents in this world are suffering because they have children. There is even a Korean proverb, "No kids, no worries."

Do not judge whether infertility is a fortune or a misfortune. Do not pray like, "Give me a baby, please." That could invite disaster. Do you go to Buddhist temple or the church?

"Neither."

Try praying like this, "If having a baby is good for me, then please let me have one. If having a baby brings me unhappiness, then please prevent me from pregnancy." Your attachment to a child, your thought "I must have a baby" is causing immense suffering. Now that you have no religion, let's just call the Buddha for convenience's sake. If you are a Christian, call God. Try to pray like this, "Thank you, Buddha. I have lived well in your blessing. I want a baby. If it is a good thing for me, please let me have one. If it is not the right time for a baby, I will just wait. I will follow the rising and changing of conditions and receive my fruits."

This is how you should pray. Do not beg or ask for something. Doing so can actually invite misfortune. Believe me, you cannot conceive a baby because it is not a good time right now both for you and your baby. If you force something, there will be side-effects. So I suggest you release your anxiety and relax. If the mother is constantly restless and insecure, even if you succeed in fertilization, something could go wrong.

Also, build some good karma. In India and Africa, there are many babies whose mothers are too poor to raise them. There are numerous malnourished children in North Korea. It costs only 30 dollars a month to raise a child there. You can be their caregiver. Send them money every month. Sponsoring those impoverished children is a merit. In Buddhism, we say you accumulate your merit. So both pray and give. Those two good minds combined can bring you good karma and hopefully a good child. How old are you?

"I am thirty-seven."

You are still young. Try praying like that for three years.

"Thank you."

Sanjusangen-do

Walking the ancient streets of Kyoto in snow.

Afraid

"How shall I live?" is a legitimate question.

"Why shall I live?" can never be established as a question.

If you start focusing on the "why," you will reach no other conclusion but to die.

I suffer from depression

A woman asked, "When I was studying in the U.K., I had severe depression. I was on medication and received therapy. I finished my degree and came to Singapore for a while. However, depression continues to seize me. I cannot get rid of negative thoughts. I keep thinking of killing myself. My parents are still alive. I know that suicide would be horrendous for them. I want to have positive thoughts and get over this situation. But when I have another bout of depression, I can't think of anything; it is just pure suffering. I take pills in extreme situations, but I can't depend on them for the rest of my life. How can I get out of this?"

If you have good thoughts, it would be best if those thoughts persisted. However, if depression sets in, good thoughts vanish. You are filled with thoughts of nihilism, of death. You cannot help it. You must always carry the pills. They can make you feel dull, but regardless, you must carry them and take them when the symptoms occur. Anything is better than dying.

If you don't have a leg, that is inconvenient but not inferior. Your condition is different. You can't do some of the things that others can. If others can do 100 activities, you can do 80. However, if you set your goal at 100, that is when a sense of inferiority arises. If you have depression, accept it as a condition of yours. It is a reality. Even if you cannot cure it 100 percent, do not be discouraged. Disappointment about a lack of improvement will only aggravate your depression.

The first thing to do is to admit that you suffer from depression. Second, modern medicine cannot completely cure depression. Third, in most cases, depression ends in suicide. Be aware of these three things. You must keep them in your mind.

However, you do not want to die, right? Now, for instance, when your symptoms are not serious, you know that you do not want to die. The problem is, when the disease is aggravated, you cannot control your mind with your consciousness. Always carry emergency pills with you. When you feel an impulse to kill yourself, take the pills immediately. Take them no matter what. That prevents suicide.

Always carry the pills. Keep telling yourself, "When it gets bad, I will take the pills." Do not think like, "These pills will not cure me anyway." At least the pills will mitigate your suicidal impulse. So when you sense those bleak and dreary thoughts rising, immediately take the pills. Do not be carried away in those thoughts. Then the grip on those thoughts will loosen and you can get out of the riptide.

The key is for you to admit that you suffer from depression. Eighty percent of patients do not admit that they have depression. That is why so many end up committing suicide. If you admit and accept that you have depression, that opens the door to healing. Unfortunately, many people will be enraged when they are told that they have depression. They scream, "Are you telling me I am crazy?"

You might think it is harsh for me to say that most of the depression cases end tragically in suicide. However, I chose to tell you so because I saw that you were ready to admit and accept your condition. You said yourself that you have depression. I deemed this approach would best help you. The most important thing, ever and always, is to understand your disease. Now that you know that your disease is depression, the risk has been significantly reduced. Depression is related to the hormones; you need medications and counselling. I suggest you get professional help from doctors. Professional medical treatment comes first.

After that, a good thing to do is to keep practicing not being sucked into the flow of gloomy thoughts. Of course, this is easier said than done, for the thoughts arise from the subconscious. The efforts from your conscious mind are often futile because the subconscious is much, much stronger. However, constant repetition in the conscious dimension can reach down to the subconscious. Then you are better able to observe depression when it arises.

Try 108 prostrations every day. Physically, it is excellent for the body. Mentally, it is a practice of letting go of the thought of self-righteousness. It has nothing to do with religion or worshipping something. You must do it every day as soon as you wake up. You have to persist regardless of whether you are sick or not, whether you feel like it or not, rain or shine. Keep repeating these three sentences as you bow.

"I feel comfortable."

"I am thankful for being alive."

"I will live well."

Repeat these three to yourself; make them burrow into the subconscious. It is the subconscious-ization of the conscious. If you are a Christian, say, "Lord, I feel comfortable. I thank you for letting me live. I will live well in your grace." If you are a Buddhist, say the same thing to the Buddha. The psychological effects are the same. Perform 108 bows every day and keep autosuggesting. This will help.

However, if the symptoms get serious, these things will not help. Have you ever been under a general anesthetic? If you take those anesthetic medicines, no matter how hard you try with your consciousness to stay awake, you cannot. The power of the mind cannot stop you from being anesthetized. I am saying that mental, spiritual things are important but the material world has its own powerful influences. If something physical is wrong inside you, you need to take medications. If something psychological is wrong, you can get psychotherapy. These two are intimately related. The therapy has to understand in which dimension the root cause lies. Physical and psychological dimensions interact with each other. You need to combine drugs with mental therapy.

Is it more tiresome to eat three meals every day or throw a few tiny pills in your mouth? Drugs alone will not cure you, but they will help you to get through this. Use drugs wisely. Emergency medications will take you past those dangerous moments. After you pass that moment, then go back to the persistent practice of prostration or praying. Hopefully a day will come when you are free from medications.

The young woman added, "My parents do not know that I suffer from depression. I do not want them to be worried. What should I do?"

You must tell them. You cannot continue to deceive them. Also, it is wiser to tell people around you. Tell them that you have depression and are on medication. People must know so that they can come to your aid when you are in an emergency.

First, it's best that you know. Second, it's good if others know. People will treat you with special attention or consideration; that is helpful.

"Is it not sad that everything is meaningless?"

Why should there be any meaning? Existence itself has no meaning. Meaning is what humans create and endow. We name this "dish," we give it a price, we sell and buy it, we use it according to its meaning. But originally, it never had any meaning. It just exists. Enlightenment is realizing that things originally and ultimately have no meaning. Meaning is made up by our mind. Useful or useless, good or evil, positive or negative, heaven or hell, or whatever. All these are creations of our own mind. Instead of staying still, humans create images, and even worse, are bound by them. They cannot help but make life complicated.

Is it not wonderful that things have no meaning? There is nothing for you to worry about. Why be sad about things being meaningless? Wouldn't it be sadder if things indeed did have meanings? There is no reason to be sad. Why are you sad? Does existence come first or meaning? Things existed far before any meanings were acquired or given. Existence simply exists; it does not have any meaning. Existence comes first; then humans come and create all sorts of meanings and play with themselves. Possession is one of the meanings that humans are particularly attached to.

One of our gravest mistakes is that we try to define existence with its meaning. Meaning came after existence; how can you explain existence with meaning? That is non-sense. For example, say you seek the meaning of life. Throughout your depression, you seek an answer but cannot find one, so you decide to commit suicide. You can reach no other conclusion but suicide because there never was an answer! Life, a pure existence, was there before any meaning arrived. The question of "Why do I live?" or "What is the meaning of life?" was raised after your life came to be. That means they do not have an answer. Then amid depression, you are likely to kill yourself from despair. You see, there is no such thing as "Why do I live?" You were thrown into this world to live. It is a given. Some people live happily, some unhappily, some freely, some tied, some painfully, some pleasantly. They all live differently. It means that "How shall I live?" is a legitimate question. On the contrary, "Why shall I live?" can never be established as a question. "How" is the question, not "why." If you start focusing on the "why," you will reach no other conclusion but to die.

Look at the chipmunks in the mountains. A chipmunk doesn't kill itself when it can't find acorns. If you kill yourself, you are lesser than a chipmunk. We do not live because life has a meaning. Meaning is what we make of it while we live. I can live on without any meaning. Meaning can make living more interesting. We can continue to make and remake meanings. I am not saying meaning is meaningless; I am saying that meaning is something that our mind creates; we should use it in a way that makes us happier.

"Thank you."

I am worthless as a mother

Nagoya

A woman explained, "I am a Korean-Japanese. I married a Korean man. He is now working in Japan. We have two children. They are in their adolescent years and it is very hard for me."

They are the ones in their adolescence; why is it hard for you?

The woman continued, "I lack confidence as a mother. I am not sure how to educate them. I don't speak good Korean..."

Dogs give birth and raise their puppies without problems. Surely, humans can do better. There is no problem. You lack nothing. You just think that you lack something. If you are not good at Korean, just talk to them in Japanese. How good is that? Your children will be able to speak both Japanese and Korean. (The lady starts to cry and attempts to sit down. The audience gives applause to cheer her up.)

Why are you sitting down? Was that all? Why is it so difficult?

"It hurts so much. I think it's my children."

Do you have any trouble with your husband? If you and your husband are fine, you rarely have difficulty with children. Tell me more.

"My daughter is too shy. I feel like it's my fault. I have low self-esteem…"

There is nothing wrong with you. No problem. What you are doing is self-torture. Do not do that. Nothing is wrong. What troubles you?

"My children worry too much. They complain all the time. They also tell me that I have done nothing for them."

What do they mean their mother has done nothing for them? If they say so, tell them, "I have fed you, washed your clothes, sent you to school. That is all I need to do and I have done it."

Look at dogs. A mother dog would milk her puppies. That is all she does. She doesn't send her puppies to school, buy clothes. Human mothers do extra work! You feed them, wash them, and school them. Just relax, laugh, and reply, "What more do you want from me? I've fed and washed you!" Why do you keep thinking you have not done enough for them?

"I feel worthless…"

Your reply lacks confidence. That is why children think likewise. Speak with confidence in your response. Ask back firmly, "What more do you want?"

Speak more. Tell me what your problem is. You opened your mouth. Bring everything out. What is troubling you?

"My daughter once said, 'Why did you bring me into this world?'"

Tell her that she is a result of love between you and her father. What is so difficult? Or tell her, "I never wanted to bring you here. You just came." Or "Why did you choose to come out from me?" If your daughter says, "Why did you bring me here?" you just say, "Why did you choose me as your mother?" Then you are even. There is nothing difficult. Keep speaking. What is troubling you? I will give you the answer.

"It is just that… my heart hurts so much. My kids vent their anger at me. They complain about their shortcomings. They are not happy with their looks."

Do you think people with bad looks will think they have bad looks? No. People with good looks are the ones who think they are not good-looking. These people think, "If only my eyes were slightly larger," "If only

my nose was a bit more pointy," "If only my chin was slimmer," etc. That is how they end up being addicted to plastic surgery. But if you had an ugly face like me from the start, you would have no desire to fix anything.

It is a general rule that those who have been praised since youth for their beauty are the ones who feel they are inferior when they meet someone prettier. If that is the case, as a mother, you need to keep telling your daughter, "It's okay. It's okay. You are pretty." Or just casually joke about it. If your daughter keeps getting stressed out about her looks, tell her that it is her father's fault. You are an adult, a mother. You should not be hurt by what kids say. It is only kid's talk. Teenagers say all sorts of things. They complain about their looks, their clothes, everything.

Is it a bad thing that teenagers rebel? No. It is a process of becoming an adult. If they are obedient, they are still children. It is very normal that they complain, rebel, and growl. Be a mother. Stay calm and just watch them grow. "My daughter is growing up." Do not say parenting them is tough. That leads your kids the wrong way. If you say your kids are giving you trouble, you are making them thankless persons. They cannot grow up to be good persons.

A mother is a mother because, despite all the hardships of motherhood, she is happy that she has children. A mother's attitude should be, "I am happy because of you. You are the sunshine of my life." That attitude will bring out the goodness in your children. Because that attitude means your children are already good people who give happiness to their mother. Raising children is no easy task: cooking food, washing clothes, schooling, etc.

However, you should always be happy to see them grow. If your children complain of their looks, just casually reply "No. No. You are pretty. No doubt. You are the prettiest in the world in my eyes." You are taking their words too seriously. You are talking to your child as a child. That is not good. Remember that you are a mother of two.

Become an adult. Having kids doesn't automatically make you one. An adult will talk to kids as an adult. You should take lightly what they say, just smile and get over it. Do not let those words linger and hurt you.

"Thank you. My daughter is here with me."

Would you give the mic to your daughter? (Ven. Pomnyun Sunim talks with the daughter) Sweetie, I am very fun to talk with. Tell me. What are you not satisfied with about your mom?

"Nothing."

Is she not pretty? (Audience replies, "Yes.") I told you. Pretty people are the ones that do plastic surgery. If you were ugly like me, you won't even dream of a plastic surgery. Okay. What is troubling you?

"Nothing in particular…"

Then why does your mom say it is so tough? (The girl starts crying.) Why do you cry? You said nothing is wrong.

"Tears... just come out."

Your tears look like that of your mother. Indeed, you are her child. Is school difficult?

"Studying is not that difficult. If I see myself... I hate myself. I am just... dissatisfied. I do not like how things are. I don't like my face. I am ugly." (Someone in the audience says, "Why? She is so pretty!")

So you think you are ugly. Maybe you have been watching movie stars for too long. Compared to them, yes, you are ugly.

See the table here? There is a microphone stand, a water bottle, and a cup. Compared to this mic stand, is the bottle larger or smaller?

"It is smaller."

Compared to the cup, how is it?

"Larger."

Then, without comparing it, just the bottle in itself. Is it large or small?

"I don't know."

Once you said it is smaller and then you said it is larger. Now, do not compare it. Just the bottle, is it large or small?

"I don't know."

The bottle is smaller than the stand and larger than the cup. So the "small or large" is a thought in the head, not something in the bottle. Your head is labeling it "small" when compared to a larger object, and "large" when compared to a smaller object. But the bottle in itself is neither small nor large. It is your perception that sometimes perceives it as small and sometimes as large. So, as you said, it is impossible to tell that the bottle in itself is small or large. So the answer would be, "It is neither small nor large." Do you follow?

If I ask, "Is it large or small?" then the reply would be, "It is neither large nor small." If I ask, "Is it heavy or light?" then the answer is, "It is neither heavy nor light." In the same sense, you would say, "It is neither new nor old." "It is neither long nor short." "It is neither bright nor dark." What exists exists. That is it. Existence is nothing more than existence. It is not big, not small. In Zen, they say "It is it" or "It is but it." Philosophically, we call this "emptiness."

You said this bottle is small compared to the stand. You think you are ugly because you compare yourself with the movie stars. If you keep doing that, you will forever believe you are ugly. If you compare this bottle only with the stand, it will forever be small. That causes a misunderstanding that the bottle is inherently small, but that is not true. If you compare yourself to a two-meter (7 feet) tall person, you are short. But standing beside a 1.5-meter (5 feet) tall person, you are tall. Do you understand that you are neither tall nor short, neither ugly nor pretty, good nor bad, smart nor dumb? You are just you.

If you study with smarter students, you will come last. If you are in a classroom with lower-grade students, you will be at the top. You are always relatively smart or not smart. So you can safely say that all things that exist are precious as they are. Things are perfect as they are.

Do not define yourself as ugly or pretty. If you believe you are ugly, that is undermining the inherent perfection you have. Thinking that you are pretty is also losing yourself. You are neither pretty nor ugly, tall nor short, good nor bad, smart nor dumb. You are just you. Things are just things.

So all things that exist are dignified in themselves. We should not discriminate. We should not discriminate against people based on their skin color, gender, sexual orientation, disabilities, and so forth. You cannot discriminate against someone for something they are born with. This is the core of the core of the Buddhist teachings. Okay. Let me ask. Are you pretty or ugly?

"I am neither ugly nor pretty."

Are you smart or not?

"I am neither smart nor dumb."

Yes! You are you. Got it? If you go to a school with lowest-grade students, you will come first. If you go to a school with only the top students, you will come last. Coming last does not mean you are dumb; coming first does not mean you are smart. Your grades going up doesn't mean you got better; going down doesn't mean you got worse. If you didn't study, but your classmates studied less, your grades can go up. If you studied hard, but your friends studied harder, your grades will go down. A test will test your relative position. My point is that you should not compare. You should treat yourself as the precious one. Harbor no thought that you are inferior or superior. Got it?

"Yes. Thank you."

To the mother I say, your daughter is a wonderful girl. As a mother, you should have confidence, for no condition can render you worthless. Your poor Korean language does not make you inferior. Your perfect Japanese does not make you superior. You are you. That is how you should think. Rid yourself of inferiority. When such confidence fills your heart, your children will finally feel at ease. They are being influenced by their mother's insecure emotions. So from now on, never think you are inferior.

Of course, do not think that you are superior either. Nothing can intimidate you. Nothing can take away your worth, your courage. If you have done wrong, then apologize. If you were incorrect, then fix it. If you do not know, then ask. There is nothing that can make you lose confidence.

What I have explained might sound simple but this is a profound philosophy. This is the essence of the Heart Sutra and the Diamond Sutra. The problem with modern religion is that the teachings of the Saints do not come down to the everyday lives of ordinary people. People go to temple or church but still live their secular lives. Their everyday worries are not addressed by religious teachings. That is because heavenly doctrines and earthly lives have not married. You have to realize that heaven and earth are one.

I am soon to become a mother
but I feel too insecure

Phoenix

A young woman explained, "I've always had a lot of fears and worries. If someone passed by, I'd imagine the person attacking me. I am even scared to ride in a taxi. I can't even answer the doorbell when I am alone. After getting married, I could manage by relying on my husband but I am pregnant now. I am worried that I might not be able to protect my baby because I am mentally so weak. For example, I am worried that I won't even be able to use a taxi in an emergency when it's just me and my baby."

You can protect your baby. Do not worry. You say you are weak but I am sure you can do better than chipmunks. Rabbits and chipmunks produce litters. They raise their young without problems. They have a maternal instinct that guides them through parenting. This is not acquired through training or education; it is something that is born with.

When you approach chickens, they run away. But when a hen is protecting her chicks, she would not move even if you come near. She would

cover her chicks under her wings, raise her comb and attack you. She attacks not because she thinks she can beat you. She is acting according to her instinct to protect her chicks. When danger approaches, a mother cares not for herself; she does everything to protect her baby.

Your fear arises from an instinct to preserve yourself. All life forms have that instinct. But when a mother has a baby, another instinct arises; that is the instinct to preserve the species. When it comes to maternity, the latter instinct supersedes the former. Any animal, when it becomes a mother, will be fearless even in the face of death in order to protect her baby.

You might not be able to conquer your fears alone. But when you are with your baby, you will have the power to defeat them. Your maternal instinct will give you strength.

However, if your fear is greater than your maternal instinct, that can actually overpower your motherhood. That may have a negative influence on the baby. In that case, you are doing much worse than chipmunks or rabbits. You are not ready to become a mother.

Having fear means you are still a child. Mothers are the strongest of all beings. To a child, the mother is God. If you observe, a mother would actually act like God. For example, if someone wakes you up at 2am at night, you'd be seriously annoyed. But if your baby cries at 2am, you rise without complaint and care for the baby. You are entirely about your baby; there is no you in that. This is unconditional love. You don't have any other thoughts, any distractions, you are purely love.

We say that God's love for humans is unconditional. So is a mother's love. But when her child grows up a little, she will start to have conditions, conditions to her giving – also known as expectations and demands. Simultaneously, or as a result, the child also develops selfishness. The baby copies the mother's attitude and actions. It will enter and form the baby's mind. If the mother is insecure, the baby will be insecure. If she has complexes, the baby will have complexes too. If she thinks she is worthless, the baby will grow up without self-respect. If she is fearful, the baby will have fears. If you have fear in you, you need to overcome them before you have a baby. Not only for yourself but also for your baby.

However, if insecurity was formed during your own infancy, it hardly changes. I suppose there would be some cause that you might or might not remember. Maybe when you woke up in complete darkness, your mother was not there. Maybe you were sexually abused when you were young. These things are ingrained into your subconscious. They generate constant fear. For instance, you feel someone is following you at night so you keep looking back. This is karma. First thing to do is to realize that you have such fear. Whenever you become insecure, do not fall prey to this feeling but instead tell yourself, "My karma is in action again. But this is actually nothing. Some bad experience in my past is creating this. But this is not real. It is empty." Consciously recognize this and comfort yourself.

Your husband needs to be especially understanding. He should not treat you like he does other people. He should give special attention to your fears. When you say, "Darling, I am so scared at home alone," he should say something like, "I will be there immediately." He should not start criticizing you. "I do not understand why you are scared. What on earth could be wrong in the house?" This does not solve the problem. Because for you, the fear is so real. As for you, since you are preparing to be a mother, you should keep reminding yourself, "I have no fears. I will protect my baby whatever it takes. I can do it." Try to cultivate this kind of attitude.

Your mind still remains at the period of childhood when you were traumatized. That experience still dominates your mind. You need a lot of practice. If you keep feeling fearful in the dark, hold the light switch in your hand, sit in the lotus posture, focus your mind, and turn off the light. Ask yourself, "Why am I afraid of the dark?" Then turn on the light. Where did the darkness go? Is the fear in your mind or in the darkness? Keep practicing until fear no longer arises in the dark. Turning on the light chases away darkness but it is the fear in you that you must oust. If you have a habit of looking back while walking in the street, make up your mind one day, "Today, no matter what, no matter how much it feels like someone is following me, I will not look back. I would rather die than look back!" Make up your mind like this and practice. Then the fear will subside.

First, recognize that you are a mother. Second, recognize that your insecurity will affect your baby, so try to overcome your childhood trauma and enter adulthood. Remember that you need cultivation to overcome the fears that you have.

What can I do to attain peace of mind?

University of California, Los Angeles -UCLA

An elderly man asked, "I am a member of the Eastern Orthodox Church. All my life, I was not at peace – physically, mentally, and emotionally. I grew up in a socialist state. The state left a suspicion in my mind about religion, about God, and the force that rules our lives. I am seventy-one years old and have not much time left. How can I find peace and live the rest of my life?"

Anyone can achieve inner peace. Whatever the experience, whatever the circumstance, anybody can be happy. The first question is realizing the reason why you are not at peace. Let me ask, why are you not at peace?

The man replied, "I do not know. I have tried everything but I cannot let go. My mind, instead of letting go, is constantly active, asking and analyzing. If I need to let go of something in order to be peaceful, I will let go. But I do not know what to do."

I suggest you approach this not in terms of what you should let go of but instead in terms of what you are holding onto. Then you can decide whether to let go or hold on. You cannot let go before you know what you are holding on to. Say you are sick. If the doctor is going to heal you, the doctor needs to know the cause of the disease first. You are seventy-one years old, live in the United States, are well-off, eat all meals, are well-dressed, and can speak English. What could be your problem?

"Those things do not help me. Exterior things are not important if I do not have peace of mind. My mind just is not peaceful. I've had insomnia my whole life. I can neither let go nor realize what to let go. Maybe it has something to do with my past. I really had a horrible past. I was born amidst the Second World War which ended when I was three years old. Then the Communists took over. It was terrible. They persecuted all religions and forced us to do what they wanted. They destroyed our souls. Maybe my mind and soul were traumatized. I don't know how to heal them."

All the things that you have said are things of the past. You keep rewinding and playing a video from the past. Stop playing it. You need to turn it off. Do not rewind it.

"How do I do that?"

Listen. There is nothing wrong with your present conditions. Nobody is persecuting your religion; nobody is threatening you with a gun. You are doing fine financially. The only problem you have is that you keep re-playing the awful memory of the past in your head.

"How do I turn it off?"

Do you agree that that is the cause of your suffering?

"It could be."

If you want to cease suffering, you should stop watching that video. If you cannot turn it off, you should watch it as little as possible. However, you keep watching it and are sucked into it. The memory of your past torments you, but you are the one that turns it on. It is best to turn it off but since that is difficult, first, try to watch it as little as possible.

"How can I not watch it?" is the question you want to raise, right? Make some effort. Bring your attention to your present. Repeat to yourself, "I am in the U.S." "There is nothing wrong with my life right now." Take a walk. Watch good movies. Try not to watch that traumatizing video playing in your head. If you can do this, although the video might still be playing, your suffering will mitigate. You say you do not want to watch the video, yet you keep watching it. Then you ask how you cannot watch it.

Next, you need to cultivate a power of peace within you that is not broken despite the playing of the video. Sit calmly, close your eyes, focus your

mind at the tip of your nose, notice the breath coming in and going out. Then you realize that the video is playing. Your mind, instead of focusing on your nose tip, is watching that movie again. Then bring the mind back to your breath. If your mind begins to watch the movie again, bring it back again. Keep doing this. It is not easy. This video is your karma; it arises from your subconscious. It is not something that your conscious can control. But if you keep practicing, your mind will grow stronger in its ability to concentrate on the tip of your nose. As time goes by, you will be able to stay focused even though you cannot turn the video off. Then you will suffer much less.

Another thing you can do is to look positively at your past. Your past was not only negative. So change the content of the video. Think again. How lucky it is that you are alive! Remember how many people died? You are so lucky. You successfully came to the United States. That is very lucky. The Communists persecuted you for your religion but they let you live. How lucky is that! Keep looking at the positive sides of your past. Then your video will change. The weight of sadness will lighten and lighten. Then will come a day when you feel that your whole experience was not too bad after all.

Try these few things. They will help you. There is not an inkling of doubt that you can become happy.

Oh, there is one more thing you can do. This is very easy. Every morning when you wake up pray like this, "Oh my God, I am alive today! Thank you so much that I live today." Pray with gratitude. This will help you

greatly. Realizing that you are alive gives you tremendous energy. Try it.

"Thank you from the bottom of my heart."

I get scared when Mommy and Daddy fight

Tenafly

A boy asked, "I get scared when Mommy and Daddy fight. What should I do?"

You can be the referee! Watch and decide who wins. Give some narration. "Mommy attacked with this word. Daddy received it and is counter-attacking with that word. Oh, poor Daddy is not as good as Mom with words. Oh no! He's starting to yell!" Just imagine you are watching a sports game on TV. There is no problem.

Whose side are you on when your parents fight? If you side with your mom, you will dislike your dad. If you stand with Dad, you will resent Mom. Neither is a good option. You want to tell your mom and dad not to fight, but that does not work. They will keep fighting regardless of what you say. But think of this. After all, YOU do not listen to everything that your parents tell you, right? Children often do not listen to their parents. You cannot expect parents to listen to their children all the time. Siding with one is no good; telling them to stop is useless.

So when they fight, just imagine you are playing the referee game. Watch them fight. At least you will get less hurt by doing so. If you start becoming sad and worried, you get hurt. That is not good. If you cannot play the referee game, if you keep crying and get scared, just go out. Do not watch them fight. Come back after they are finished. The best method is to be the referee. The second best is to just go out.

You wish your parents never fought, right? But you see, it is natural that people argue. You will understand better when you grow up. If you are traumatized by the fight between your parents, that is not good. You will have negative notions about marriage that continues on into your adulthood. Your mom and dad fight with each other but they do not separate; they live together. Why is that?

The boy said, "Because of me."

Yes. Your mom and dad might have arguments. But they love one another. They are giving you love. They feed you, raise you. You feel thankful, right? Do not side with any of them. Be grateful to both of them. Do not think one is right and the other is wrong. It would be really, really good if they did not fight, but in this world, you see, you cannot have everything your way. Never become saddened by their fighting.

How can I become confident?

Pittsburgh

A young man asked, "I got my Ph.D. last year. I am looking for a job as a part-time lecturer. My biggest problem in life since youth is that I lack confidence. Even in my own eyes, I look childish. I make silly mistakes every day. People around me reproach me all the time, 'Can't you even do that?' I try to enhance my self-respect, but that is not easy. I tend to depend on other people – like my boss or my professor. When I am praised I feel nothing but as soon as I hear 'I gave you a chance. Is that all you can do?' I completely freeze up. Then I get all worried, so I can do nothing. I want to become independent and do well but I never could since my youth. Social life after becoming an adult is no easier. How can I increase my confidence? Or how can I stop relying on others?"

There could be two causes for this problem. First, as a child, you grew up with your parents or others scolding you all the time. You were not encouraged. You were rarely told warm words. That has become a trauma. If that is the case, you can get help from consultations with experts. You can find when such trauma was formed, and start healing it. You may lack confidence not necessarily because you are incompetent but because the trauma from your past keeps haunting you. It is ingrained into your subconscious; it continues to belittle you. It looks strange to other people because you are flawless on the outside – smart, well-educated, have a job – yet you seem to be insecure. You have many things people would normally envy, yet you yourself feel inferior. The cause mostly comes from childhood experiences. So you need to find and heal it.

Second, it could be your greed. If you have 100, a result of 80 is good enough. However, you seek to be over-rated beyond what you actually are. If that is the case, then results will never please you. You always feel that the grades are unfair; they do not accurately reflect your worth. You feel that how your boss or people around you speak about you is not correct; they never meet your expectation level. That is why you lose confidence.

You have to let go of this excessive expectation, this greed. That is the biggest problem. You said that you have no confidence, you think you are incapable. Then how did you make it to a Ph.D.? Objectively speaking, you were a smart student in school. Were you within the top five students in primary, middle, and high schools?

"Yes."

You were within the top five but you were frustrated because you were not number one. Number five is still superb, but the thought that you were not number one made you feel inferior. Think about plastic surgery. Do ordinary people do it more or the movie stars?

"The movie stars."

Movie stars are already beautiful or handsome. Why would they do plastic surgeries? Not-good-looking people like us don't even consider doing plastic surgery. But those celebrities, even though they are already good-looking, have dissatisfaction about their looks. They want larger eyes. They think their nose needs a lift. Then they don't like their round chin. Inferiority complexes are not found within people at the very bottom, those who you actually think would have them. It is the second-best, second-place people, those who outperform the average, who carry the complex.

You are working as a lecturer. You might not be praised as the top lecturer by everybody, but still, you did something better than others so that is why you got the job. You have too many expectations, greed. You look only at what you do not have. That is why you seriously undervalue yourself. Lower your expectations. When your superiors say "Can't you even do that?" just say, "I will do better next time!" Remember that you hear those criticisms because you have a job. Aren't many people jobless? High expectations give you big disappointment; low expectations give you little dissatisfaction.

If the reason is because of the first case, trauma formed in your youth, that is not easy to fix. But if it is the second case, think thoroughly and positively and you can fix it. You obtained a Ph.D. in America, wrote a dissertation in English. You are already a competent man. Be positive about yourself.

There is one more thing to consider. Discrimination has been abolished legally, but in real life, it persists. It is human nature to want to give privilege to friends, family or people from the same school, hometown or country. The U.S. is a mixture of diverse ethnicities and cultures. Birds of a feather flock together, remember? You are a minority here. Of course, if you experience clearly unlawful discrimination, you can go to court. But there are things that you have to tolerate as an immigrant. The culture is different. If you don't agree with that, go back to Korea. You will be in the majority in Korea.

For example, say someone belonging to the mainstream in the U.S. has a competency rated at 100. People will likely admit that the person has 100. But if you are an immigrant, you have to understand that you probably have to be 120 to be recognized as 100. Consider this as a given. Strive to increase your skills. Do not despair in the given social conditions. Please tell yourself that you are doing good already and accept any perceived unfairness as natural.

I want to have a boyfriend,
but I have no confidence

Sacramento

A female student asked, "I am twenty-five years old but have never had a boyfriend. I like boys and am interested, but I do not seem to have the courage."

If you had observed yourself about why that is so, you might have known yourself better. But you do not seem to have taken the time to look into yourself. There could be many reasons. First, your expectations might be too high. If you regard the boy you like as a prince, you are likely to lose courage in approaching him. The boy should not feel to you like a prince. He should feel more comfortable to approach. Don't try to find the perfect man.

The young woman replied "I don't think that is the case. All the boys that I had liked already had girlfriends."

That means that your standard is high indeed. Just pick a boy that no girl has picked up. If all the cool guys already have girlfriends and you only like those boys, that means your standards are too high.

For example, let's think about job selection. It's likely that smart people get so-called good jobs in large corporations or become doctors or lawyers. Those jobs are very hard to get. Not everyone who wishes can become a lawyer. If you think you can, that means your standard is too high. Then you cannot find a job. You might think working for Samsung is no big deal, but it actually is.

If you are thinking that your boyfriend should be working at a Samsung-level corporation, even if you find such a boy, it will be very difficult for you to approach him. You may also have fear. If you think about it, do you remember becoming nervous when you met people with high status, like a very rich person or a celebrity? You get all the more nervous when you want to make friends with them. They are not easy for you to talk to or make friends with. So bring down your level of expectation. Then, there are many, many boys in the world.

The second possibility is that when you were little, your parents had some kind of serious conflict. You have grown up and might look okay on the outside, but your subconscious might have a problem with men. That is because it remembers the terrible fight that went on between your parents. Also, when a mother comes back weeping from a fight, holds the baby and says negative things about her husband, that is imprinted into the baby's memory. It does not matter whether the baby understands or not. The baby will develop hostility towards men. Those women, when they grow up, can fall in love. However, when they try to take their relationship the next level – get married for example – something in them will resist. They keep feeling fear. It is out of their control. The mind continues to be troubled. This could be the second case.

Third, you may have experienced a horrible experience of sexual abuse when you were little. You might have forgotten about it after you grew up, but that experience would have instilled repulsion or fear of men in you. Look back at yourself for these possibilities too. You have to know yourself why you have fear.

You might have seen your friends meet boys, love, but then separate at the end. In bad cases, they not only break up, but become enemies. You might have thought, "That is terrible. I won't have any boyfriends!" That kind of thinking is very wrong. It is only natural that in some cases you are disappointed at the other person although your first impression of the person was quite nice. Breaking up is not a bad thing.

Meeting a person, getting to know the other person, is a gradual process. A woman might like the man because he was staunch, manly and charismatic. But after marriage, what used to be attractive could turn out to be a disastrous quality. She could eventually come to completely detest the man's stubbornness and machismo. Some ladies fell for a guy because he was sweet and caring. However, the guy turns out to be too soft, unable to make decisions. Then the girl is disenchanted. Can you see that we ask too much of the partner?

We sometimes want our lover to be sharp as a knife, spongy as cotton, hard as a rock, or soft as water. So when they first met, they were immediately attracted to some visible characteristics. But as time went by and they spent more time together, they found that there were this and that and other less-visible but unexpected and undesirable characteristics. That is why they break up. It is much better to break up while you are lovers than after you have married. If you already married, it is much better to break up before you have kids.

Say you met a guy for the first time and immediately got married to him. Then you missed out on so many opportunities. You'd regret because this is the twenty-first century. You cannot meet new guys after marriage, right? So in the long term, before marriage, it can be quite beneficial to meet many guys. Don't be afraid of the man leaving you. If you are the one that was abandoned, nobody will think you were the nasty one. After you break up, you can meet a new person.

Don't be hurt by guys leaving you. Don't be afraid. This can actually be a good thing. If the guy leaves you, just tell him, "Good-bye. Thank you for leaving me." Then breaking up won't be as traumatizing to you. If you have a boyfriend, that is good. If he leaves you, that is still good. What is there to fear? Put down the worry. Meet boys.

If you start disliking the guy, you can just say good-bye. Look how high the divorce rate is. Breaking up with a boyfriend is not a problem at all. The boy might not be happy. But never mind. You didn't even like him anyway. Don't worry so much about how he feels. If he leaves you, that is okay. If you leave him, that is still okay. Whatever the case, there is no problem.

Why am I going on like this? I want you to realize that you need not feel any anxiety when meeting guys. Let me speak a bit more about this subject.

The problem is that people take it too seriously when they meet a boyfriend, girlfriend or someone to marry. If you are too serious, you will start being picky. You can't just love or marry anyone. You look at their age, education, occupation, and so forth. If you start filtering out men, you will feel that there are no worthy men in the world. You do not realize that the problem is in your own filter, your greed.

I advise you not to be too purposeful in approaching guys. If you are determined to make him your lover, the guy might feel uncomfortable. Would you not feel the same if someone pinpointed you with a purpose and approached you accordingly?

How should you approach others? First, it is good to begin as a friend, not as a lover or a fiancé. You shouldn't have a determination to make this newcomer a boyfriend. Meet many different people. Don't worry if the guy is twenty years older than you, is married, twenty years younger than you, is divorced. Just make friends with a wide range of people. You will have a much wider pool to choose from. You can start a serious relationship if you find someone. Start the love. If he leaves you, that is good; if he doesn't, that is still good.

Meet three or four guys like this, then you will understand men much better. If you are over-passionate, the boys might hold back and lose inter-

Jeong-Hae Elizabeth Korean Catholic Church

est. Also, if you are too cold, the boys will bounce off. Actually younger generation calls this "pushing and pulling." This is not something that you do with a plan – you just naturally understand how it is done with some experience. You will become especially good at it after a few failures. If you enter into a serious relationship with a man after these processes, you will be much more mature when you finally do get married. Inexperienced people face more difficulty in managing relations. This can be perilous in some cases.

Angry

People have different thoughts and behaviors. They are just different.

It is not that one is right and the other is wrong.

There is no right or wrong, good or bad.

I have to be with someone I hate

/

Ottawa

/

A man said, "I was born a Christian and still am. I wanted to under-stand more about Buddhism, so I started studying it on my own. I was deeply moved reading about the 'suffering from having to meet those whom one hates,' which is one of the eight universal sufferings. I guess I felt this way because I have had many of these experiences. Can you please tell me about your experience and give me advice on how to over-come this suffering?"

It is indeed stressful to have to meet someone whom you hate. It is hard enough when you hate a stranger, but if the person whom you hate is some-one you live with, that is a serious suffering. Another form of suffering that pairs with it is "suffering from having to part with your loved ones." This, on the contrary, means that you want to stay together but cannot. So on the one hand, you have suffering from not being able to have what you want, and on the other, from having what you do not want. This applies not only to you but universally to all people.

The emphasis of this teaching does not necessarily lie in explaining that you are destined to part with your loved ones or meet those whom you hate. Rather, this refers to the suffering that necessarily arises from love or hatred that you have within you. Subjectively, you can either like or dislike a person. Objectively, you can either be with or without a person.

There are four cases. If I like someone and am together, there is no suffering. But if I separate from the person, then it hurts. If I am separated from someone I hate, there is no stress. But if I have to meet this hated person, that is a torture. What can you control? Can you control the given conditions?

Events unfold as they are conditioned. You cannot change that. You cannot control how you meet and separate with others. That is something already preordained. You may like or dislike having to meet someone. Likewise, you may like or dislike having to separate with someone.

You cannot control whom you meet or do not meet. Ultimately, you have to change that which is subjective. You have to break free from both the loving and the hating mind. That is why the *Xinxinming* (Faith in Mind) begins with the phrase:

The great way is not difficult.

All you need to do is to neither like nor dislike.

Stop loving or hating

Then it will become evident.

This does not just reference the love between a man and a woman. It teaches us that we should avoid both like and dislike.

What is the best practice in such situations? It is leaving the conditions as they are, yet changing your mind. You change it so that it is no longer bound by the conditions; it is free.

If you have to meet someone, be free from hatred. If you have to separate, be free from love. When we are greedy, we try to bend the exterior conditions to our liking. However, conditions arise and recede according to their own terms, not according to our desires. Practice is about accepting what is as what is. You release the desire to have something. You even release the desire to release.

Desire arises from karma, or habit, or propensity. If you can let go of it, all defilements will go away, and you will become free. This is nirvana or moksa. There are two types of freedom. One is being able to do as you please, being able to do something according to one's desire as in the slogan, "Give me liberty or give me death." But this freedom is only achieved when the appropriate conditions are met. This freedom is about getting what you want. Therefore, this kind of freedom is always imperfect and half-fulfilled at most. The second type of freedom is the perfect, absolute freedom. It is not about getting what you want; it is about being free from what you want. Complete freedom is being free from oneself.

So there is the saying, "It is easy to defeat an army of a thousand, but difficult to conquer my one mind." What does "mind" mean here? It is desire, emotions, habits, tendencies, memories, stored energy... all together called karma. Simply put, practice is becoming free from karma.

Let's say you hate your husband. It is easy to divorce him, but not easy to divorce your hatred. First, you have to be free from your own self. Like or dislike is something of your own making. You make it up according to your karma.

Karma can be defined as the subconscious, ignorance, or habitual reactions. You get mad without knowing. You burst into anger by habit. You hate without a second thought. The three refer to the same thing. When someone is addicted to drugs or tobacco, their craving arises automatically. Karma is the same. Emotions arise according to the tendency that we have instilled in ourselves. Much of our subconscious is formed when we are babies or children. Do not believe that yours is "the right" view or try to change the world to suit your taste. I am not saying you should eliminate all your emotions. I am only saying that you should understand how all this works. Then, you can start walking the path to liberation.

I learned a great deal in the 1980s when I was arrested and tortured by the military government that ruled South Korea at that time. Of course, I was not the only one to suffer in that dark period of history. Many activists, scholars, opposition leaders, labor unions, and students were also persecuted. One day, strangers broke into my house. They put a bag over my head and took me to an interrogation camp. They beat me without reason and urged me to confess to my crimes. I did not reply and then they started to torture me. They insulted me, calling me all sorts of names. They struck my bare feet with a baseball bat. They applied immense pressure to my spine. They covered my face with a cloth and poured water on it so that I would suffocate. I struggled and yelled. I wanted to faint to escape the pain but that was not easy. It was so painful that I just uttered anything to make them stop the torture. However, the comedy inherent to that whole situation was that I had no information they wanted in the first place, so I could not please them no matter what I said. Whatever "answer" I gave was not what they wanted. So they would go back to verify my "answer" and come back angry, to torture me even more.

You cannot imagine the enormity of the anger that grew inside me. I was arrested, beaten, and tortured for no reason, for doing nothing wrong. The rage was like a fire in me. It burned like crazy. I thought to myself, "Just wait until I get out of this place. I will kill you all." Terrible as it may sound, that is actually what I thought. If I had had a gun in my hand, I would have shot them all on the spot. I did not only because I could not.

Do you know how strong a human can be? When your life is at risk, you will become incredibly strong. The torture brought out all the power I had; it took three big men to hold me down for I was yelling, screaming, struggling, and wrestling. It must have worn them down. In between the torture session, I sometimes caught sight of them taking a rest. They would smoke and speak of casual affairs. One day, I overheard one of their conversations.

"My daughter is taking the university entry exam today. I am so worried. I hope she can get into a good university in Seoul. I am worried about how to pay for her tuition too."

That is what the torturer said. Other torturers said something in reply which was in perfect accordance with what and how "ordinary" people would speak. They were talking of things in a manner exactly the same as normal people. Just a moment before, I had no doubt that they were demons. I was extremely shocked. I realized that when they finish work and go home, they are no different from any other fathers, husbands, and sons. They might even regard themselves as patriots. Maybe they think they are doing a good deed. Their wives might have cooked nice, warm meals for them, and praise them for their hard work. The daughter would come back home that day to her father, give him a hug, and talk about how the exam went. They were normal people.

Suddenly, I understood one of the messages of the Holy Bible I had read years ago. When I was little, I could not understand that part of the book no matter how hard I tried. I thought of Jesus. Jesus forgave the people who killed him. How great is that love? What about myself? Those torturers did not and were not intending to kill me. But what did I think? I was ready to kill them. The immensity of love that Jesus showed was purely beyond human. That was the moment when the anger and hatred vanished within me.

Being tortured is an indescribable pain. But looking back, compared to all the meditations I did, I probably learned more through that experience. Maybe luck does not always come in the form of luck. If you are wise enough, you are able to grasp the fortune disguised as misfortune. Ultimately, you can say, "There is nothing that is not a blessing."

Some people like to pray asking for favors. They ask God for something. When their wish is granted, they say it was by the grace of God.

When not fulfilled, they say God abandoned them. This is not a true faith. As a human, you are ignorant. You do not know whether having your wish fulfilled is ultimately good or not. If you really receive God in your heart, accept that only God knows everything and is capable of everything. Leave it in God's hands. Whatever the result, it is God's design. God is good. As a human, all you should do is to give thanks.

Practice is entrusting everything to God. Pray that, "Thy will be done." That is same as Buddhists saying, "Letting go of self-righteousness" or "Things arise according to conditions."

I hate my father

/

Amsterdam

/

A woman said, "My mother took her life nine years ago. My father married another woman just one year after her death. I keep feeling guilty when I think of my mom. I can't help stop hating my dad. My heart is cold toward him. I have not visited Korea for the last nine years. But now my kids are growing up, and they want to visit Korea. I want to take them to Korea but I do not feel prepared to have them meet my father."

Your father belongs to a different generation. He has lived a different life, in a different setting. It is not his fault that your mother died. Your mother made her own choice. Even if that originated from a conflict that she had with your father, that does not necessitate such a radical decision. Not all couples who fight end up in one side's suicide. Do not blame your father. The conflict that your mother had with her husband is only a condition. If she took her life, I believe she was suffering from depression. Genetically, it is likely that your mother's mother also had the same disorder.

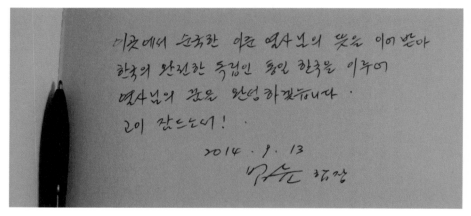

이곳에서 순국한 여러 열사님의 뜻을 이어 받아
한국의 완전한 독립인 통일 한국을 이루어
열사님의 꿈을 완성하겠습니다.
그이 잠드소서!
2014. 9. 13
법륜 합장

We will carry on the dream of Jun Lee,

a patriot who gave his life here seeking liberation of his nation from the Japanese colonial rule.

We will strive to bring forth a peacefully reunified Korea,

for that is the true realization of liberation that he dreamed of.

Rest in peace.

Sep 13, 2014

Pomnyun

You might have that same potential too. The reason I say this is because you should understand yourself correctly so that you do not blame others, your husband, or the environment, but look straight into your fate and stand up to it. Tell yourself, "This is my karma. I will not be sucked into it. I will be victorious."

Your mother, as unfortunate as it might be, has made her own choice. You should let her go. Say good-bye. Your guilt and sorrow do not bring her back. They only kill you. If you keep holding on to your emotion of sadness and grief, your mother's soul cannot leave you. If she does not go where she should, she becomes a "lost soul" that forever wanders around you in this world, instead of moving on to the next. This is a seriously bad thing for you to do to your mother. What does sorrow do for you, for your family, for your mother? Why do we traditionally have a funeral on the third day of death? It is because, after three days, you should stop crying. Why do we then have a 49 day ritual to conclude the funeral? Because Buddhists believe that on the 49th day after death, the spirit enters a new body, and thus gets ready to be reborn. So 49 days is the maximum period that you are allowed to grieve. After that, do not weep anymore. You have to let her go. Let her go so that your mother can be free, so you can be free.

When your mother died, your father ceased to be her husband. It is his freedom to choose another woman of his liking and marry at a period of his liking. Old or young, beautiful or not, rich or not, it is his right to choose and live with a woman of his choice. I understand that you might not be happy with that, especially because you feel sorry for your mother.

But remember, your father has his own life; he has the right to make his choices. He did not abandon your mother. Why do you intervene and judge him? You are not being fair to your father. What your father chooses is none of your business.

Do not judge others with your views. Do not expect your father to be a great man of your making. I suggest you go to Korea immediately. Take your kids, show them their grandfather and have fun. Meet your father's new wife, call her, "Mother," make her happy, and have fun. Give her gifts. Give your dad hugs. You make your own prison and cry out in pain. You restrict your own travel and lament your confinement. You are free to go to Korea. You are not a criminal banned from entering the territory. Are you going to keep staying in the prison? (Laughter.)

I cannot forgive my mother for leaving me

Union Theological Seminary in the City of New York - UTS

A lady said, "My mother left me when I was little. I lived with my cousin until I was twelve years old. After that, I lived with my sister. At eighteen, I became independent and had to make my own living. I met my mother after many years. She was seventy-five years old. I asked her why she left me. I demanded an answer. But she was too old, and I could not believe that she was telling the truth. I cannot forgive my mother. This hurts a lot.

Also, I have no goal in life. I think that everybody should have a goal, but I find it difficult to have one. I tried to become an actress, but my sense of purpose was not strong. And now, every once in a while, I remember the awful memories of my youth and break down in tears."

You say you were abandoned by your mother. You were abandoned in the past, but you are abandoned no more. You are not in an abandoned state. It is your thought that you were abandoned that is tormenting you.

Your source of suffering is not here in the present, but in something that happened in the past.

Your body is here with us in the present, but your mind stays ever in the past. It is like a person watching a movie. People die in the movie, but that is no problem. Turn off the TV. In your head, you keep rewinding and replaying a painful scene in the movie of your life. You are intensely focused on that experience. Just like getting sad when you think of a sad movie, you break down every time you remember your past. When you do not cry, it is because you have come back to the present.

You must always be awake in the present. Stop watching that movie called "The Past." It only brings back painful memories. You cannot live your life watching a movie from the past over and over again. Look around you. There is nothing wrong with you at the moment. You are alive. You are healthy. There is no reason why you cannot be happy. It is your playing that movie from the past that brings you suffering. If you want to suffer, keep playing it. If you do not want to suffer, stop the movie. Discard the video tape.

Of course, the problem is that even though you want to discard them, they do not go away easily. You keep going back to the past, keep replaying that awful scene and immersing yourself in grief. This means you need to make some effort. Whenever your thoughts drift back to the past, bring them to the present. When you sense you are going back to the past, I suggest you immediately focus on the tip of your nose. Feel your breath going in and out. Feel that and feel alive. This breathing, this in and out, this is

Union Theological Seminary

the present. If you are awake in the present, there is no suffering.

What is important is the choice you make. You can either choose to keep playing that tragic movie from the past and continue spending your life in grief, or awaken and live happily in the present. This is not your mother's problem. You cannot imagine the pain of a mother who has abandoned her child. I suspect there should have been some difficult circumstances your mother encountered during that time. It is natural that when you were young, you could not understand your mother. But now that you have grown up and are at the age your mother was in the past, you must understand your mother's situation at the time she abandoned you.

Your mother gave you life. You should be grateful. If it were not for her, you would not be here. So pray like this, "Mother, thank you for giving me life." Pray only to express thankfulness. Then your future will get brighter. Thinking of the past only consumes you. Being attached to the past makes you helpless; being worried about the future makes you restless. The past has already passed, and the future has yet to arrive. Always be awake in this present, this passing moment.

Also, the experiences you had in your youth were not all bad. You said you wanted to be an actress, right? Let's say you received the role of a girl abandoned in her youth. You would be the best actress for that play. Everything you have experienced can become a great asset for your future. Whether to keep these experiences as an asset or a liability is your choice. What will you do?

I repeat. Anybody born to this world can be happy no matter what the experiences were in the past. The Buddha said, "Everybody can become a Buddha." So you must realize how precious an existence you are. Live happily. Be happy.

I regret my feelings after getting mad

Budapest

A middle-aged man asked, "I work for a Korean company in Hungary. I have a lot of stress working in a culturally different workplace. Sometimes I do not understand Hungarians. I find myself getting angry a lot. I get mad, and after that, I regret it. How can I control my anger?"

So, simply put, you have a bad temper. (Audience laughter.) If you have a bad temper, you can either live with it or fix it. If you choose to live as you are, naturally more people will dislike you. That is the consequence. So if you decide to stick with this temperament, then you have to pay the price. If you don't want to pay the price, then you have to fix your temper.

However, this "temper" is not something you can easily control. It arises from deep within you, from the bottom of the subconscious. It is not easy to fix. It may seem that this "anger" arises out of your control, and can never be controlled.

So, your first choice is to live as you are, because it is extremely tough to fix it anyway. But then, people will dislike you.

Second, if you choose to fix your temper, then you have to realize that it requires super-human efforts; for example, a shock therapy. If you give yourself a life-threatening pain every time you get angry, your subconscious will kick in and fix your temper — out of a need to survive. For instance, you can buy a Taser gun and shoot yourself whenever you realize that anger has overtaken you. You'd rather live than get angry! Taser yourself just three times and then next time you are about to explode, you will find that your mind has become as docile as a sheep. If this sounds too harsh, try three thousand prostrations. Prostration is an excellent method of practice; three thousand repetitions is mighty enough to crush any ego. It is so exhausting that your subconscious would never want to do it again.

Third is a therapy of gradual practice. Keep practicing controlling your anger until non-anger becomes your habit. Do 108 prostrations every day; every time you do it, tell yourself, "Anger never arises in me." Here is a hint for autosuggesting. It is better to say "anger never arises" than to say "I will not get angry," because the latter involves invoking your will-power to do something that is hard for you. If you "fail" to control your anger, then you will be disappointed.

Instead, keep reciting, "Anger never arises in me." This is better. "Anger never arises. Nothing triggers anger." Every time you feel anger arising, be aware of it immediately. When you observe yourself about to get mad, tell yourself, "I need not be mad, don't go crazy," and the anger will die down.

If you cannot fix your anger issue, you will suffer not only in your workplace but also in your family – and your family will too. Your mar-

Budapest Capitol

riage will run into crisis. If you have children, they will start to imitate you. That is a terrible thing. So, I suggest you do 108 prostrations every day, and keep telling yourself, "There is nothing to be angry about."

This will help you a lot. But again, if this doesn't work, you can always buy a Taser gun! (Laughter)

I am kind to strangers,
but I easily get mad at my husband and children

A lady asked, "I find it very tough to say 'no' to others. When they ask me for a favor, I almost always comply. I just cannot decline other people's requests. This causes me a lot of stress. I think that is why when I come home, I vent all my anger at my husband and children. On the other hand, when my husband asks me for something, I rarely listen. I know this is bad, but I cannot help it."

You have given the answer yourself. If you cannot help it, you cannot help it. You see, changing your personality is a near-impossible thing. If it was easy and you were able to do that, you would not be here asking this question.

The first thing you have to admit is that it is extremely difficult to change your personality. You are trying to change something that is hardly changeable. Naturally, that causes you stress. Stress caused by others is another matter, but causing yourself stress is the first thing you should avoid. Accept the fact that it is hard to become a different person. That is the starting point.

Not being able to say "no" is not necessarily bad. Most people find it too easy to say "no" and that becomes, in many cases, the source of social conflicts. Not being able to say "no" actually contributes to the resolution of these conflicts. We need more givers, helpers, and understanding people in this society. Did we not, as Buddhist practitioners, pledge that we would give love rather than seek to be loved? Cheer up. You are closer to a saint than anyone else. (Laughter.)

There is a truth within you that you have to face. Why can you not say "no"? It is because of your greed. You have a strong desire within you to be seen by others as a nice person. You want them to think you are a good, kind, giving person. You want to be loved. But you are foolish. Is it better to be loved by strangers outside your house or by your family inside the house? Doing all sorts of favors, sacrificing, spending your time and energy for others – what good did that bring you? Try doing only a tenth of that for your family, and the response from your husband and children will make you jubilant. Look, observe, and realize the fact that you are not as good a person as you think you are, or as you want others to believe you are. You are just wanting to be loved and recognized.

I am not saying you should be mean to others. I am saying that you have to deal with your desire for love. Look, Jesus was killed because people of his era did not understand – let alone recognize or approve – of him. Buddha was also a great man, but he suffered from all kinds of slander and censure. Are you greater than them? Why do you seek to be entirely un-

Poklonnaya Hill

derstood, well received, and plentifully loved by everybody, which even these great men failed to do? Your excessive desire makes you tired. Your goal is too high. It is impossible to attain. Being recognized by others, being loved and respected – these are powerful desires we have, sometimes even stronger than the hunger for money or power. Do not be stressed out by such things. And don't pass on that stress to your family.

So, the next time someone asks you to do something for them, do it happily or decline. When you decline, brace yourself for harsh words. They may even curse you behind your back. I am not saying you should be hated. I am saying that you should not try to have everybody love and praise you all the time. You are on an arduous journey of pretending to be a person you are not, a person nicer than who you really are. This can be a big source of suffering.

You cannot have it all; you cannot achieve everything. If you can get something, that is fine. If you cannot, that is also fine. That is how it is. Do not be mad, angry, or frustrated at failures. Do not think that you can do for others everything they want. You cannot even do everything that you yourself want. Do what you can, what you are happy doing. The rest? Say "no."

Of course, people will be frustrated when you tell them "No." But their reaction is something you have to accept. It is as much a delusion to believe that you can satisfy other people's wishes as it is to believe that you can fulfill your own desires. That is impossible. What you can do, do it happily. What you cannot do, tell them you cannot do it. Practice phrases such as,

"I do not have time," "I can't do that," or even, "I don't want to do that." Coming home and transferring that stress to your husband and kids is the worst thing you can do.

Now, put yourself in your husband's shoes. Probably one of the main reasons he married you was because he saw that you were nice to people. Perhaps he had expectations that you would be kind and caring to him. Now that he's married to you, you've changed. You are no longer that anxious-to-please type of person anymore – or at least not to him. Some men are like that; they are nice to others but are terrible to their wives. This kind of character is hard to fix.

Again, finally, I am telling you it is not that you are such a nice person that you can hardly say "no;" it is because you have a desire to be liked and accepted. That is greed. Now that you have discovered the reason for your inability to say "no," you may let go of that greed.

What do I do when anger arises

Athens

A man explained, "I get angry easily. It happens unexpectedly, out of my control. For example, I get pissed off when I see a car that doesn't follow the traffic light. And then I always regret having gotten angry. I want to know how to control my anger."

Try 108 prostrations every morning. Tell yourself, "There is nothing in the world to be mad about." That will help you. You see, what happens is what happens. That has nothing to do with your anger. You yourself, always, trigger the anger in you.

There is nothing in the world to be mad at. So if you are mad (angry), indeed you are mad (crazy). Tell yourself when you are about to get angry, "I am about to go crazy. Let's not do that." Anger is indeed a light degree of madness; it is not normal. If someone attacks you with a knife, a sane response is to run away. But if you are mad, you stick out your tummy and shout, "Go ahead, stab me!" You can see that anger is a type of madness.

First, if you give in to your anger, what happens? You are angry at someone and express your anger. Then the other person becomes angry in return. So anger feeds on anger and keeps growing. This is the least wise of choices.

Second, if anger has arisen and you suppress it, that does not inflate anger, but it will definitely make you stressed out. Suppressing your anger is never a good method. If you can suppress it, you may be respected socially, but you will suffer greatly personally. So this is not so wise either. This path has nothing to do with liberation from suffering. A good practice is never stressful. You do not say you practiced well because you succeeded in suppressing anger. You have practiced well only if you have not fallen prey to suffering. Buddhism talks about the perfection of perseverance (Kṣānti pāramitā). It is not about a great suppression of anger. It is about there being nothing to suppress.

Third, you can notice yourself immediately when anger arises. Be mindful. Catch the moment. Tell yourself, "Wow. You are about to get angry. You are about to go crazy." People have different thoughts and behaviors. They are just different. It is not that one is right and the other is wrong. But everybody unknowingly makes judgments based on their own desires and preferences. Humans always perceive the world based on what they see. Because they themselves are at the center, something different from them becomes something wrong. Eventually, when faced with someone different from their ideas, they say, "I am right, you are wrong." If someone is doing something "wrong," that has to be fixed. But the other person does not think that they are wrong, so they do not fix it. Seeing

Acropolis of Athens, ancient city of Gods

Reflecting the history of greed of Gods,

exploitation by humans

this, naturally, anger results. "You are wrong. Why don't you fix it?"

I suggest that you first understand this theoretically. There is no good or bad. There are only differences. All you have to do is to recognize and accept them. Then there will be no reason to get mad.

However, we still keep placing ourselves in the center. It is a tendency ingrained into our subconscious. When that happens, again, immediately take notice, and say, "Oh, you are judging things as you please again. You are being a dictator." Do not suppress yourself. Only take notice. Then breathe deeply. Do not let anger speed up the pace of your breath. Concentrate on strengthening your mindfulness of the situation. This may not completely eliminate the anger, but it will help. Gradually, if you got mad ten times a day, that will come down to nine. Practice more and it will come down to seven. Before, you might have been consumed with anger for an hour, but gradually, it will pass after 10 minutes. You will improve fast.

Whenever you get mad, tell yourself, "You are going mad again. You are claiming you are right again." Caution yourself. Do not focus on outside things. Look into yourself. This is where meditation helps. Meditation trains you to be aware of your own state.

My mother and aunt were very close before but are now enemies

Montreal

A young lady explained, "I was only fourteen when I came to Montreal alone. I lived with my aunt and now am twenty-two years old. However, something went wrong between Auntie and me; we are not close anymore. I moved out and started to live by myself. I sometimes pay my aunt and uncle a visit, but I am still not comfortable with them. Last year, I was going to travel to Korea to visit my parents with the money I had saved, but my aunt and uncle were adamantly opposed. They said, 'If you have money, use it for your tuition.' My mother and aunt have become mortal enemies now. What should I do?"

As for the relationships between your mother and aunt, do not worry about it. They are sisters, and it is a sister thing. You are indeed indebted to your aunt, but that is that. Since you have grown up and are an adult over twenty years of age, you can live freely according to your choice. A mother has to raise her kids until they are twenty years old. Your mother neglected her duty and left the rearing of her daughter to her sister. That is something that your mother has to pay back to her sister. But what you need to know is that you have nothing to do with this business. It is not your fault, not your responsibility, not within your capability. Just live your life. If you miss your auntie, go pay her a visit. If you do not like her, do not see her.

Before you were twenty, you were not an adult and could not decide on your own. Whether it be your aunt or mother, your guardian had the authority to decide. But now that you are over twenty, you are an adult who can make your own decisions.

There is a paradox in life. When you bring in and raise a child that is your brother's or sister's, you likely end up becoming enemies with that brother or sister. Your aunt is not a bad person; but has fallen into that trap. She might love her sister greatly, but still, it is not an easy task to raise a sister's child successfully. Look now. Is she not her sister's enemy? Is she not always fighting with you? Your aunt made a bold choice but, sorry to say this, she seems to have failed. There is a reason why brothers and sisters often become enemies if they take care of their sibling's children. I suggest you try to have some compassion for your aunt.

There are two difficulties in raising someone else's child. First, children want to do whatever they want. Auntie will try to bring in some discipline and scold the child. Who does the child go to? The child will tell his or her parents. Who does the mother listen to? The child, of course. Then what does her sister have to say? She calls the mother to tell her how much of a problem the child causes, how awful the child is behaving. No mother in the world will like to hear that. If your aunt was smarter, she might have chosen not to scold the child at all. Then what happens? The mother will come back at her with a different kind of anger, "I trusted you and thought you would educate my child as if she were your own. Now you have spoiled my child!" Both choices will come back to haunt the good-willed guardian. Your aunt is not a bad person; she has become a victim of this dilemma.

Your aunt is the biggest loser in this game; you have lost nothing. Do not resent her. Remember to thank her. Your aunt might have been harsh with you or might have stuck her nose in all your personal affairs. But I will tell you, had you lived with your mother, you would have had no less stress. You might be feeling hurt about your aunt's actions. But your aunt acts that way because she feels like your mom. You resent your aunt's actions because you do not accept her as your mom. Whatever the case, try to remember that she raised you. You should be forever thankful. She has done no wrong.

The person suffering the most right now is your aunt. She spent eight years raising you, giving you love and care, and now you have deserted her. She thought she did her best for her sister, but now her sister hates her. Whatever she says, just tell her, "Thank you," or "I am sorry."

Because you are now an adult over twenty, you can choose a life of your liking. You do not have to listen to your aunt. But you should remember to always be grateful to your aunt for having raised you. You did not grow up by yourself. Always keep a thank-you in your heart. Go see her and help her. You live your life; you are the master of your destiny. You do not have to be bound by your aunt anymore, but do remember to be grateful for the love and care she has given you in the past.

My mother keeps criticizing my father

Munich

A woman asked, "It has been three years since I lived in Germany. I work during the week, so I call my parents on the weekends. I usually talk to my mother, but every single time, our conversations end with her criticizing my father. I get so angry that I always end up hanging up on her. But this situation repeats time and time again. Why is my mother like that? Why can't she change? I get really stressed out every time I call her."

You have seen your parents argue since when you were little. For twenty years, they have continued to fight. Their pattern of fighting has hardly changed over two decades. Do you think it will ever change? Parents cannot change their children. How can children change their parents?

First, you are stressed out because you desire what is impossible. Why do you want to have something that you cannot have? You are seriously mistaken if you think it is possible to change your mother. Of course, it would be best if your parents stopped quarreling. But that is your hope, a

San Marino

mere desire, wishful thinking. There are things you can dare, want, aim, and many things that you cannot. Their issue is theirs, not yours.

Second, is it not strange that your parents, after all that fighting, still live together? Your view is that there exists a burning hostility between your mom and dad, and it is almost impossible for them to live together. But why then do they stick together? For twenty years! Maybe the problem is seen as a problem to you but not to them. You see, it is normal that husbands and wives fight. They love, they fight, they fight, they love, and so they live.

Then what should you do? The situation? Let it be. Your worry? Let it go. When your mom calls you and starts blaming your dad, just say, "Yes, Mother." Do not listen only to your mom and then start judging your father. If you start labeling your mom as good, or as the victim, and your dad as evil, or as the culprit, you will start developing a sense of resentment towards your father. It is not good to hate parents. Empathize with your mom, but do not join in the demonization of your father. The problem with many children is that they base their judgment on their mother's words alone and arbitrarily define their father.

Likewise, don't try to speak for your father either. Don't yell at your mom saying, "Can't you stop! Can't you see that it is because you are so nasty that Dad has no choice?" You see, parents are stubborn creatures. Funny, they always chastise their children for not changing, yet they themselves never change. Your mother is looking for a place to vent, to let out steam. She is not bowing down to you asking for some great teaching. If you start preaching, you will be just another version of her husband in her eyes. What option would she have then but to treat you like she does your father? The best thing you can do for your mother is to listen without judging. Just say, "Oh, Mom, that must have been tough."

Children should not step into their parents' fights. Just leave it be. They are adults. If you want something positive to come out of it, then learn from their experience and remember that you will never fight with your spouse in front of your children. You understand the distress it brings to the children. Make it a valuable lesson. Understand that it is possible for adults to fight, but that really has a bad influence on the children. However, do not try to solve your parents' problems.

If you have the power to change your parents, then do so. If you have such powers, then I beg you to change all those politicians too. Politicians fight far more seriously than your parents. Why do you let them fight and not let your parents? (Audience laughter.)

Just thank them. Despite their disagreements, they did not break up, and they managed to raise you. That is something to be grateful for. Even if they did break up, still thank them. They gave you life. So next time you answer the phone, greet them warmly, and you say this first, "My beloved mother, I am so happy you called. I am dying to know who won this time." (Laughter.) Do not let this situation sadden and consume you; conquer and shine through it. It is your smile, your light-heartedness that helps your parents. If you stay upbeat, your mom will finally give in and start laughing with you.

But if you try to act as a mediator and side with either your mother or your father, that will be a bad choice. Don't try to teach them. Don't try to coach your mom. Your mother just wants to talk; she does not need a solution from you. Listening is good enough.

Desirous

You will be as happy as you deserve, not as you desire.

Only as much as your karma permits.

How do I renounce greed?

/

Google

/

A man asked, "You said that to be happy, one must renounce greed. That is easier said than done. How can we do that in our everyday lives?"

If it is difficult to give up your craving, you can choose to hold on and consequently suffer. If suffering becomes extreme, you might let go.

Say this object is hot. How would I react when I grab it? "It's hot!" I'd exclaim and let go. But instead, what if I keep holding on and yell, "It's so hot! It's killing me!"? Someone tells me to let go. Then do I ask "How do I let go?" This doesn't make sense. It is not because you do not know how to renounce greed that you cannot let go. It is because you want to keep holding on that you keep holding on. If you want it, you need to burn your hands. If you want to keep your hands unharmed, you have to let go. It is not a matter of how to let go.

Teaching is simply saying, "If it's hot, let go." In Buddhist terms, we say "*Banghachak*," simply meaning, "Put it down."

However, people keep asking how they should let go.

This is a strange thing to ask but the teacher has to give an answer so they reply, "Move it to your left hand." Then the questioner will be satisfied and say, "Why didn't you tell me before?" Because the person can both keep the object and save the right hand. But soon the left hand will start burning. Then the teacher says, "Put it on your knees." This is a good solution but again only temporarily, because now the knees start burning. Is it wise to keep shifting the hot object? You might eventually put it down, but all the process was unnecessary. You have to understand the essence of this matter. It is not because you do not know how to put it down; you simply do not want to put it down. You are holding on and screaming that it is hot. It is such a plain truth: if you want it, take the pain.

But do we want a painful life? No. Then we should let go. Of course, I understand that people find it difficult to let go. Say a smoker asks, "How can I quit smoking?" Then the answer is, "Quit smoking." Do you see the point? Many smokers miss the obvious point. They keep asking how they can quit, but in essence, all they are saying is nothing other than that they want to smoke. This is a habit. It is in the subconscious. It is not solved overnight.

You have to choose between the two. One, give an overwhelming shock to your subconscious. Say you promised yourself that you will never let anger overtake you. This is not easy. If you really want to fix it, buy a Taser gun and shoot yourself every time you fail your promise. Such a shock will surely leave an impression on the subconscious. Just repeat five times and then as soon as anger starts rising, your body will already be shaking. But in reality, people don't want to resort to these extreme measures. They actually do not feel that much of a need. Whatever they say, they are not so desperate. That is why they fail to fix themselves.

Two is a method of sustained practice. A practice should not end in 3 days; it should go on for 100 days, 1,000 days and so on. Then the conscious will enter the subconscious. Anything that has aged with time becomes a habit. Habit means subconscious. This can be seen in the law of physics. What has been moving wants to keep moving. What was static wants to stay still. That is the law of inertia.

If you apply a large force to stop a moving object, it will stop quickly. If you apply a small amount of force, it will take longer to stop. So either you use great force (shock therapy) or small force (gradual practice). The problem is that people rarely do either. That is why karma ever continues, reproduces, and grows. We believe in fate because people hardly ever change. For example, the Chinese people believed in the Four Pillars theory [from the Book of Change, where the four pillars of year, month, date, and time of birth determines one's fate]. Indians understood this as karma from previous lives. Christians saw it as the will of God. These views or expressions were established based on the notion that changing destiny was impossible.

However, all things change. Karma is something that has been formed. It can be formed otherwise, it can change. But if it was formed over a long time, change is difficult. A karma formed in youth is harder to change. So you have to either give a shock or engage in relentless practice. Then anybody can bring about change. The thing is that people choose to do neither. They want their lives to change but they do nothing. They make some small one-off effort and quit. I suggest your will-power should be either enormous or continuous. Then anybody can change.

It is your consciousness that registers knowledge. Generally, knowledge cannot bring about any change. But if some knowledge touched your heart and you cried, change is more likely. Because at that moment, the knowledge reached your subconscious.

In sum, first, you must fully understand that greed indeed is the source of suffering. Second, if you want to escape suffering, you need to let go of the greed. Third, greed originates from the subconscious so is not easy to change with will-power or consciousness. To destroy this habitualized greed, you either have to give a powerful shock or continue a sustained practice. Then the change will come.

I cannot approve
some qualities of my children

Portland

A mother asked, "I have three daughters. The first and second have completely different personalities. The eldest is self-centered, less empathetic, is not considerate, and boring. The second daughter is too soft, too giving, is not strict with others, and lives in a fantasy. I usually fight with the eldest. Her character is not without advantages, but I am worried that she does not have that human warmth.

The second daughter is actually quite happy by herself. I am a bit worried that she might not adapt to this real world, whether she will be sociable or not. When the eldest and second meet, it is war. The older sister launches a major attack on the younger. Watching that, I get mad at the eldest. I feel I have to protect the weak. But when I am not around, she really is a devil to her little sister. How should I look at my daughters? How can I bring balance between them?"

I need to point out a fundamental flaw in your view. You want to have all the good things. A knife is sharp; cotton is soft. Since the knife is sharp, you use it as such; cotton is soft so you use it as such. You are saying, "The cotton is soft so it is useful but it cannot cut things. I want it to be sharp." Or, "The knife is good for slicing food ingredients but I also want it to be soft." These demands can never be met. This is called greed.

If your eldest is rational, help her use that quality for the benefit of herself. If your second is soft, help her so that that quality may help her in life. When your daughter complains of flaws in her character, you should give her courage. When she says "Mother, why don't I have sharpness?" then you should tell her, "Darling, you have softness. A person cannot have everything. What you have is good enough." As a mother, do not start saying, "That is a serious problem you have." If a girl is not even recognized by her own mother, how can she be recognized in society? You should be on your daughter's side. Even if people were to point out something bad about your daughter, you should be on the defensive, arguing, "Your view is not necessarily right. I've raised her and I know her wonderful qualities." Like this.

But you have already reached a conclusion that, "My daughter is hopeless. She lacks this. She has that problem." What more is there to do then? What room is there to maneuver for your daughters? As a mother, you should be a nurturer of your own children even when others criticize them. If your child has a physical disability, it could be called greed if you try to make the child the same as ordinary people. Because that is impossible. If you try to do something impossible and force your child to comply, the child will be traumatized. She or he is likely to develop an inferiority

complex. When a child with a disability tries to become same as others, a good mother would tell the child, "Darling, you don't have something that they have. But you have such good qualities that you don't need to try to be like them." Then the child can be happy because they correctly understand the reality and accept themselves as they are. Give encouragements. "You can be happy as you are." Those words will make your children happy whether they are physically or mentally disabled or not.

Actually, the main reason why children develop an inferiority complex is because of their mothers. When their children have a disability, some mothers lament, saying, "What bad karma do I have from my previous life?" This means that the mother is actually thinking that the disability is a punishment. This is not in accordance with the Buddhist philosophy of emptiness.

There is no good or bad. All things that exist are precious. Whatever the skin color, the sex or sexual orientation, everybody should be respected as they are. However, when PARENTS are the first to disapprove of their children's differences or disabilities, the children will have very little chance of developing a good sense of self-respect. As parents, you should be the first to accept, encourage, and protect your children.

There are four things that you must strictly educate your children with. First, you have freedom but that does not include the freedom to hurt others. You cannot harm or kill people. Second, you are free to seek profit but that does not mean you can freely damage others' property. Do not steal or scam others. Third, you are free to love but not free to coerce others. Sexual assault, harassment, or violence is unacceptable. Fourth, you are free to speak but you cannot use your speech to harass others. Do not lie or slander.

These four things are the absolute essentials to live with other people. No matter how little your children are, make sure you teach them these. If you fail to do that, your children can become evils in this world and live unhappy lives themselves. Apart from these four, refrain from making any right-or-wrong judgments and forcing them on your children. Let them live freely. When they grow up, there is one more thing: teach them not to get drunk. It is okay to drink alcohol, but it is a problem to be intoxicated. If you get drunk, you are more likely to commit all four sins.

If you compare humans with animals, all humans are similar. But if you compare humans to humans, you will notice differences. Some people are more emotional, some more rational, and so forth. I have seen human psychology classified into sixteen different types.

Grab a handful of beans. They all look similar. But take a closer look – they are all different. You can find thousands or even millions of differences. But again, you can also say they are one and the same. When you look closer with a smaller lens, you are able to identify the differences.

What you are born with should be agreed with. In Buddhism, we say, "All sentient beings are Buddhas." There is a beautiful phrase in the Bible that says we are God's offspring. Everybody can be happy. This wisdom was taught more than 2,500 years ago but it is still not fully received by humanity.

Do not see problems in your child, see promises. The eldest has her merits, so encourage her. The second also has her strengths so spur her on as well. Do not start judging who is right and who is wrong, who is better or worse. However, if anyone does not comply with the four laws, then you should reproach them firmly. You can see that there are principles to education. The problem is that many mothers just scold their children as they feel like. In particular, the worst thing a mother can do is compare their children with others. If a child did something wrong, then talk about that specific wrong she did. Don't say, "Can't you see that your sister is so nice? Why do you misbehave?" This does serious damage to your children's psychology. This method of speech is discriminatory and irrational; arises from a mother's state of unstable psychology. This is the perspective I can offer you.

"Thank you. My head is much clearer. I feel my thoughts have become more flexible."

I see that you understand what I have said. But understanding does not necessarily bring about a change in your behavior. Behaviors are based on habits, habits formed over a long time. Also, it is really important that when you get angry with your daughter, you should immediately realize, "Oh, I am becoming emotional." Keep practicing and you will get better at it. Do not let your anger dominate your communication with the child. When talking to your child, do not act according to your temper. That will do serious damage to the child's healthy emotional development. If you feel your anger rising, immediately leave the child, go outside, and take deep breaths. Only after you have calmed down should you talk to your child. Do not be swept away by your emotions. Do not fight with your child. Do not shout at or suppress your child. Such acts will cause turmoil in your child's psychology. They may even boomerang back to you in the future. There are children who, after growing up, actually assault their parents. This is not the sole fault of the child. It can be the result of inappropriate parenting that has destroyed a human being.

How can I meet good people?

A student asked, "I am seventeen years old. I am planning to go to Ko-rea to enter a university in two years. I am looking forward to meeting many good friends in Korea. How can I meet with good people and build good relationships?"

There is no such category as "good" people. Whoever you like is a good person. They are good if they are good to you. If others think the same person is bad, then that person is bad for them. The person in itself is neither good nor bad. It is just a person.

Separating good from bad people is an error. You are wanting to believe the world as you perceive, not as it is. In other words, you will be objectify-ing your subjective views. So you are asking me, "How can I commit an er-ror in perceiving the world?" That is not right. You should rather be ask-ing, "How can I overcome errors in my perception of the world?"

If you wear red-colored glasses, the world looks red. If you wear blue glasses, it's blue. This "It is red" or "It is blue" perception arises because of the lens that you wear. This color of the lens is called the karma. In modern terms, a karma is our habit of perceiving objects, the structure of our thought process.

Your perception and other people's perception are different. Christians see things differently from Buddhists. Their paradigms are different. Koreans see history differently from Japanese. For Koreans, the period from 1910 to 1945, when the nation was annexed by Japan, is one of the darkest eras in history. That is why, for Koreans, *Junggeun An* who assassinated a Japanese leader in 1909 is a hero, a patriot who fought for independence against Japanese colonial rule. For the Japanese, he is just a terrorist and a murderer, who killed one of their leaders.

Once you take off your glasses, you will realize, "Oh, it was not red after all!" "Wow, the world was not blue!" Things are immediately clear. Recall the stanza that all images are not images? This realization that "I see that the world is not what I see" is what the stanza is talking about. The path to enlightenment is realizing that there is no such thing as red.

Does that mean we should all take off our glasses? No. It is okay to leave them on. Should the world appear white to us? No. It is okay to see it as red. The key is that when it looks red to you, you must realize that it looks red to your eyes, not that the world itself is red. If the world looks blue to someone else, that person needs to search within themselves about why it is so. That means that there is no need for conflict should there be a difference in views. Try cultivating understanding and tolerance by, for example, switching glasses. "I see that you can see it differently." "I see that my husband can see things differently." "I understand why my mother sees it like that." These are good attitudes.

This is the path to understanding. "I understand that your habits are such, thoughts are such, beliefs are such." First, admit that you and others are different. Second, understand the other. "I understand that in your circumstances you can see it this way." This is the path to peace. Look around. People fight wars for peace. Hatred is excused under the name of love. You must realize that love without understanding is just another violence. Do we not see everywhere "love" manifested in the form of violence? Look at domestic violence. You give love when you feel like it but when that feeling is no more, you turn to hatred. You love someone who is nice to you but as soon as the person is no longer nice, you are enraged. You have to be careful when meeting people. They might be like angels but they can turn into devils as soon as you do something they do not like.

So do not try to separate good from bad people. Just because someone is to your liking, that does not mean the person is good. The person is perceived as good to your eyes because of your karma. If you believe someone is bad, it does not mean that the person *per se* is bad; it means that your karma is in operation to make them look bad to you. If you realize this, you will make fewer mistakes. That is how you can meet many friends. Do not be bound to the idea of good or bad, for they are generated by your mind. You do not necessarily have to take off your lens and see things in white. We see things as red or blue in our lives. Our perception is established according to our karma. It would be best if you could see things as they are from the beginning. But this is possible only when you have completely eradicated your karma. In Buddhism, we are called sentient beings. All sentient beings are restricted by karmas.

When a mother has a baby, she is repeatedly told to be careful in her parenting. That is because an ego is formed up to the age of three. This ego, formed at early age, will persist throughout life. It is because karma has become one with the ego. That is why, since ancient times, people have said that people do not change.

Think of this "temper"— the kind of temper that we talk about when we say, "That guy really has a nasty temper." Temper is very hard to fix. It is an old habit. The way we generate liking or disliking results from our habits. In psychoanalysis, we call this "the subconscious." Our conscious mind is the basis for reason. Our subconscious is the basis for emotions. This is how we are made. We need to know this.

When you feel bad about someone, do not simply say, "That person is bad." Instead, realize that your karma makes you see things in a certain way. Do not say, "That is red." Only say, "That looks red to my eyes." Then you can make friends with everybody in the world. If you understand this thoroughly, you will never make enemies. Your karma can make you think of someone as either good or bad, or it can make you shift from one judgment to another. This means you are becoming a slave to your karma, which can represent a serious flaw in your relationships. But just because you understand this in theory, it does not mean you will not make mistakes again. As I told you, your subconscious has not changed, and karma stems out from the subconscious. However, there is no choice for us but to keep cleaning ourselves of our karma, keep getting out of our subjective errors, keep waking up from delusion.

As a Korean who grew up in Central America, you have a different karma compared to Koreans in Korea. Even inside Korea, those from the east region are different from those from the west. Koreans from different families are different. You may be excited about returning to your home country, but soon you might be confused because you cannot understand these people. In that case, remember what I told you. "I see that this person sees things that way." Don't say someone is bad. Just understand that the person has certain habits or tendencies. That is how you make and maintain good relationships. In the end, you will have good people around you.

How can I be loved
as a wife and as a daughter-in-law?

Madison

A young woman asked, "I am getting married in two months. What attitude should I have in order to be loved by my husband and my mother-in-law?"

The love you seek is what your mother-in-law and your husband give. It is what they give, not what you take.

"My parents-in-law should have some expectations when accepting me as their family. Can I ask them about those and make efforts to please them?"

That can be a way. But why do you want to be loved?

The lady answered, "I just want to be loved. I did not grow up in a loving family. I visited my husband's family last summer, and I could see that the atmosphere was much different from mine. They were happy. I was delighted that I should be one of them. I came to believe that my family will be a loving and happy one."

I see how much you would wish that. But you have your karma. Wherever you go, your karma will dominate. Things will turn out as your karma has laid out. It is not impossible to change a karma, but it is extremely hard.

The young woman said, "Do you mean I should live in unhappiness?"

I did not say that. I just said if you are thinking, "I will be loved as a daughter-in-law, as a wife," that is not for you to decide. You will be as happy as your karma permits. You will be as happy as you deserve, not as you desire. Wherever you go, your karma will rule.

Plant a bean in Korea; you get a bean. Plant it in America; you still get a bean. It does not turn into rice. I am not trying to discourage you; I am trying to tell you facts. Then you make your choice. However, do not base your question on ignorance. You cannot escape your karma. If you desire for something that is not given, your marriage cannot be happy. It does not matter whom you marry.

What should you do then? You should give love. If you want to be loved, you should give love. Love your husband and your mother-in-law. However, loving to be loved is not love. It is better than wanting to be loved without giving love, but still, it is a "trade." It is basically the same as investment where you seek a return. What did the Saints teach us? "Give love without seeking to be loved."

"I don't know what love is."

Love is just being happy at the other person's presence. Say you like being in the mountains. Have you ever asked the mountain to love you back in return? No. So there is no problem with loving the mountain. But when you love your husband or mother-in-law, you are asking for a return. That expectation is turned into disappointment. So you must love only and not seek to be loved.

Say you love a flower. It is you who is happy with the flower, not the flower. If you love your husband and mother-in-law, you are happy. If you love the world, you are happy. If you want the world to love and recognize you, you will fall into despair. It is good that you asked this question. If you did not have this knowledge, your marriage would likely have failed.

"I understand that I should give love first."

It is not enough that you understand. You should be very careful here. It is true that if you want to be loved, then you should love. But if you love with the purpose of being loved, that can result in dissatisfaction. Because the love you get in return might not be to your expectation. You have a 50 percent rate of success when you love and seek to be loved. You will fail 100 percent if you do not love but only seek to be loved. You have a 100

Leaves change colors in Madison city

Fifty-ninth Dharma talk out of one-hundred

percent rate of success if you do not seek to be loved but just to give love.

Do not seek to be loved. Because even if they love you, their love will never meet your expectations. It is very dangerous that you should visit your family-in-law and think, "Wow, what a loving family! I will be loved so much here!" For example, when you are invited as a guest and the host has prepared delicious food, are you going to think, "This family eats delicious food all the time. They must be rich!" No. They only prepared the food because a guest had come.

Why do marriages fail? Young people nowadays are careful, they check each other out, try living together for years, but still, they often end up divorcing. Why? Because they expect too much out of marriage. If the expectation is high, disappointment is bound to be high. Such a relationship cannot last. So I tell you: Discard all fantasies about marriage. Prepare yourself for adversity. Give up all your rights when entering a marriage. If you cannot give them all up, give up at least half. Only then will your marriage be successful.

The young woman then asked, "It seems that to let go of greed is of the utmost importance. How can I practice doing that?"

First, you have to realize that you have greed. When you have trouble, do not blame others but realize that it originates from your greed. Do not say, "How can you do that to me?" but rather "I was greedy." Always watch yourself. Watch how your greed generates problems. You do not even have to try to fix it. Just notice it. When you are angry, the problem lies in the thought, "I am angry because you did a wrong." Not many people realize, "My bad temper made me angry again." This turn, this critical turn is what you need to make. If you can do that, evil does not spread. It may still arise, but it will not grow. It stops there.

You need to realize your thought beforehand, "Oh, I have such high expectations. This can create conflicts after marriage." You must understand that greed can turn you into a not-very-lovable type of person. Have no fantasy about being the most loved person in your new family. Rather focus more on how you can be of help in the new family, how you can help your husband and so forth. Do not be disappointed at your husband when he turns out to be someone different. He never changed. You never saw it.

Acknowledge the difference that exists between you and your husband. Then you must be ready to change yourself to suit your husband. Some ladies ask, "Cannot the husband change himself for me?" Well, that is for the husband to decide, not for you to ask. All you should ever think of is bending yourself for him. Then you will be happy. Your problem is that since young age, you have not seen and learned how people give love. So it can be difficult for you. Since childhood, your subconscious has been used to sticking only to your needs. You have to realize that. Observe yourself and understand that. Regardless of your religion, I suggest you do a lot of prostrations. Look and realize how attached you are to your needs.

I want to live to serve others

Raleigh

A student asked, "I chose to study public administration for my post graduate studies in order to help people and bring about a better world. When I chose this path, I had forsaken wealth. I also knew that no matter how hard I tried, there would be little chance for real change in the world. I want to run a non-profit organization in the future. I am sure I will have no regrets. I want to know what the source of your passion is. You have lived your life for the rights and happiness of others."

When you compare living for others and harming others, the former might be slightly better, but fundamentally, the two are not much different. You can harm others for your own gains. That is the worst thing to do. But you can harm yourself for the gains of others. This is also very bad.

People say if you harm others for your profit; that is evil. If you harm yourself and benefit others, people call that good. However, this kind of good deed cannot be sustained. Harming others cannot continue because the victims will inevitably resist. Harming yourself also cannot persist because there is a limit to tolerance. The only sustainable way is to benefit both oneself and others. Therefore, what you must keep in mind is that if your starting point is, "I will sacrifice myself for the good of others," then there will come a time when you regret it. You will be sorry for the life you have lived. You will lament, "I have sacrificed for my family, for my country, for this world, and what have I gotten in return?" This is dangerous. You can end up despising the world, cursing your country, blaming your family, and eventually hating yourself.

Your starting point should be, "Doing this is good for me. I like it. I prefer it." If you can succeed in what you desired to accomplish, that is good. If you cannot, that is still good. There is no failure. You have done what is good for you.

Do not hastily judge success or failure. Bringing about change takes a long time. If building up ten bricks is the goal, I am likely to build up two and die. Future generations or my descendants will come to pile up two more. When they die, their later generations will come to stack up two more. It will take five generations to accomplish the task. If you have a larger goal, then it will take even more time. If you set up a small and practical goal, you can succeed just tomorrow.

Do not think that you should live for someone. From what I hear from you, your mind is infected with an "I-am-a-good-guy" disease. If you keep that thought, you will start fooling yourself. Do not over-estimate your life. A human is a mere trifle being. Rabbits and humans are the same in that they both are born and then one day die. Do not think of a human life as something grandiose or epic. Do not endow too much meaning to your life. You said you study public administration. Eventually, you will have to make a living with that knowledge. Do not keep thinking that you are doing something great. Be grateful for what you will get to earn. It is the same for marriage. If you have an "I am sacrificing for you" kind of attitude, the couple will fight forever. If you think instead, "Thank you for living with me," then there will always be peace.

Being able to earn a living is a blessing. Waking up in the morning without dying at night is also a blessing. Think light. "Wow. I am alive. Let me do some good while I live." Do it casually. This kind of light-hearted approach is what I suggest. If you have too great a burden on your life, you will become stifled. Do not live under such enormous pressure.

The student then asked, "I thought getting angry at social issues was a motivation. Should I not do that?"

I understand you getting angry. However, remember that when you get angry with someone, you produce destructive energy. History sometimes needs destructive power, such as in the times of revolutions.

But is Korea or the U.S. in need of a revolution? A revolution destroys all institutions and builds them anew from scrap. This is not the period for that. Now is a time for ongoing reform. Be positive about the world and criticize. This will bring reform. If you base your criticism on negative views, you will generate destructive energy.

Look at history. Most revolutions fail to resolve things. This is because the revolution destroys but does not create. Out of ten revolutions, nine fail. The one that succeeds does so because there exists a creative power within the revolutionaries. In the Chinese revolution for example, a figure like *Zhou Enlai* possessed a great degree of compassion. He was not all rage. Because of such a person, the revolution did not fall into radicalism. If you are negative, there is a risk of becoming radical. The rage also destroys you from within. You will be overwhelmed by despair or hatred.

Korea has both positive and negative elements. Maybe positive to negative is 51 to 49. Even if positivity is greater by only 2, I still think it is time for reform, not revolution. You have to first recognize the positive sides of Korea, and then discuss what to improve – like democracy or welfare or whatever. You should not give in to your anger and destroy all establishments. Social movement based on rage tends to destroy. This is not good. Elevate that energy. Keep practicing so that you may transform your anger into positive energy.

Look at Korea, look at us; we are not without problems. We have the descendants of collaborators of Japanese imperialists still well off. There are super far-right extremists. There are all sorts of people. But they all have a right to vote. Your heart must be such that you can embrace them all. Only then can you produce a positive energy. If you tilt toward hatred, you cannot bring about lasting change. A movement based on hatred easily buckles to despair. I believe a transformation of energy would be useful.

If you have a lot of anger, do many prostrations. Much anger means much self-righteousness. Bow down, lower your head, and touch the ground. Then you will be able to better release that grip on your thought, "I am right."

I want to live a giving life

A man explained, "I lived in Australia for the last twelve years and lived with foreigners even before that. I had struggles and disagreements. I went through all sorts of troubles. I realized that I had a sense of inferiority because my family was not wealthy. I had lots of jealousy, rage, and hatred. I often cursed other people. However, after learning your teachings, I have repented. I want to live a good life. But my life in Australia was all about competing with and defeating Australians. I studied harder and worked harder. I felt that if I didn't take it, nobody would give it to me. But the more I took, the more I wanted.

I want to change now. I want to live a giving life. All your lessons, I can understand with my head, but when I try to give, my hands will not open. I suddenly think 'How hard have I worked to earn this money? You were lazy when I was working.' This thought troubles me. Please help."

Then hold on more. Greed drove you in your making of money; now it is greed again that is driving you in your giving away of money. Whether it goes in or out is different, but they are the same in that they are greed. Say a secular person is a slave to greed. That person would do anything to get rich. But all attempts have failed and he is out of business. Now, he is interested in the divine world. He comes to the monastery and becomes a monk. Then the person again becomes a slave to greed and decides, "I will practice very hard and I will become a Buddha!" Whether such a person's body resides in the secular or the divine world, the soul is delving in greed all the same.

You said you pursued money doggedly and now you regret it. You do not need to be hasty about letting go. Do it slowly, step-by-step. Do not try to give away everything at once, but give little by little. If you give all and become empty, you might suddenly be overcome by an urge to refill again. Just live comfortably; give only as much as you feel comfortable. This is a practice. You are practicing giving. For example, if you ignored beggars in the streets before, now give them 50 cents or 30 cents; do not give 100 dollars. If you offered 10 dollars to the temple before, increase it slightly and offer maybe 20 dollars. Do not try to increase it dramatically. Give gradually; the most important thing is that it makes you happy.

What you need, it seems, is to be calm. You are too excited. You heard my teachings and you want to give everything away immediately. Giving everything is not wrong; I am saying that you are likely to regret it in the future. You might think, "What did I do! I was crazy! Why did I listen to that monk!?" So what you need to do right now is to be calmer. Calm down and start giving slowly. You might be enraptured after learning of the Dharma, but calm the mind and settle down. Start giving after that. If you want to make an offering of a large sum of money, do it three years later. Make sure you leave no regrets. If you act out of hastiness, you are likely to experience regret. Calm down and keep practicing. Slow down your life-long tendency of pursuing money. Slow down with that pursuit first; then start to give. When your mind has calmed and is clear, then it is a good time to start giving.

The man said, "I understand. One more thing. Can you please give me a prayer?"

Certainly, as you prostrate, tell yourself, "I was greedy all my life. I have realized that greed is causing suffering. Now, I am thankful for just being alive. That is the attitude with which I will live."

"Thank you."

Dissatisfied

You are the one who is serious about your problem, but you have created it.

The problem is problematized by you but in reality it is not a problem.

There is no problem; there is no need for suffering.

Why am I so unattractive?

A woman asked, "I want to ask you about unfairness. Why am I only 150 cm (4 feet 9 inches) tall? Why am I not good-looking? Why are there rich and poor people? Why are there happy and unhappy people? Is there some natural law? Was the world meant to be so unfair?"

If you are born in a society with serious gender inequality where men have more privileges, then you can understand why women lament being a woman. But if the world were fair for both sexes, such questions would never arise. Being a male or a female in itself has nothing to do with good or bad; it is the social structure that privileges one over the other that makes women regret being born as women. I am saying that it is not because of some bad karma in your previous life that you are born a woman. It is not God's punishment either. Your question arises fundamentally because there exists sexual discrimination in this world.

Let's look at disabled people. These people with physical disabilities face discrimination in their everyday social lives. So they have this question in their hearts, "Why was I born disabled? Did I do something wrong in my previous life?" Again, I emphasize that it is not the sin or karma or any wrongdoing of these people that made them be born as such; it is the sin, the evil, the wrongdoing of our society to have let such discrimination fester. Now, the problem is that religions, taking advantage of this, develop evil theories. They say, "You are unfortunate because you do not believe in God," or "You committed much evil in your past life." These statements are wrong.

Go back to the original teachings of the Saints. Did Jesus or Buddha teach us to discriminate against people based on gender, the color of their skin, or disabilities? No.

Now, back to you. You think that "being tall is good and being short is bad." This kind of thinking is wrong. Tall or short in itself cannot be labeled as "good" or "bad." What is tall is tall; it has its own merits. What is short is short; it has its own virtues. An elephant is larger than a mouse, but that does not mean it is superior. They are just different. This person's face looks like such, that person's face looks as such. That means that the two faces are simply different – one is not more handsome than the other. The idea of what is good-looking is something transitory, something formed and changing according to the custom and perceptions of the people living in a certain period.

Inequality based on artificial thoughts and custom is not real. Any difference that exists in nature is natural. That is "difference," not "inequality." In nature, you see, there is no inequality. A snake hunts and eats a frog.

Does that mean there exists an inequality? Is the snake better off than the frog? No. They just belong to different species. We are born with different skin colors naturally. There should be no discrimination or inequality based on that.

We need a revolution in our perception. What we perceive and accept as beautiful shall undergo a radical reform. That is why some came up with the slogan, "Black is beautiful" to fight racial discrimination. You can change it to, "Short is beautiful." Think of all the advantages of being short. You need less food, consume less energy, and use a smaller bed. (Laughter) You are being nicer to the environment. Do not look at things with a good-or-bad notion, but rather with things-are-simply-different attitude.

I love my family,
but they don't love me back

A lady said, "It's been twenty-five years since I moved to Portugal. I have many siblings. Among the eight brothers and sisters, I was the youngest. Our family was loving, we always talked to each other a lot.

As an aunt, I am very giving. I always send gifts to my nieces and nephews on their birthdays. I think I am lonelier and attach myself more to my family bond because I live overseas. But recently I came to realize that it was only me that loved my family. I did an experiment this year. During the Thanksgiving holiday, I intentionally did not call anyone. I expected a few people to call and ask me if I was well. But nobody bothered. I was very hurt and sad. I feel like I am becoming petty. This has been bothering me so much that now I cannot even sleep properly."

You are unhappy because your investment is not giving you returns. You feel your investment so far has been in vain.

Look back at yourself. You want a return on your investment. You are not sure whether you should continue to invest when it is not giving you any profit. That seems to be your major consideration. People have a similar attitude towards love. They give love, but if they are not loved in return, they easily resort to hatred.

However, think of this. You might go hiking to a mountain. You go there once, twice, and thrice. The more you go, the more you get to like the mountain. But has the mountain ever loved you back? Have you ever gotten mad at the mountain for not returning your kindness? You keep loving the mountain regardless of its silence. The mountain might be indifferent to you, but you can still love the mountain. It is a one-sided love.

You look at a flower and marvel at its beauty. "Wow, this flower is so beautiful!" Who is happy? The flower or you? You are happy. In Lisbon, you see the Atlantic Ocean and shout, "Wow! This ocean is awesome!" Does that make the ocean happy? No. You are happy. When you love something or someone, then you are happy, not the object.

If you love the mountain, ocean, forest, or God or Buddha, you do not expect to be loved in return. So this love has no problem. However, when we love another human being, we almost always expect something in return. "I have given love ten times, then should she or he not give back at least once?" This inner voice makes you suffer. It comes from you. It is not your sisters or brothers, nieces or nephews who are making you suffer. You see, suffering originates from within you. Now you are on the verge of exploding. You give off warning signals all over. You threaten them, "If you don't love me back, I won't love you. I will stop investing!" But your family is not catching that signal. This makes you all the more perplexed.

When do you make a phone call? Do you call when you want to give something or when you need something? Ninety percent of the time, we call because we need to make requests, ask for favors or questions. The telephone was invented so people could ask for favors from each other. So it is always the person in need who makes the phone calls. There is a saying, "No news is good news." If there are no calls, that means all is well. If someone makes a call, it means the person is in need.

Your brothers and sisters in Korea have lots of friends and lots to do. They would be communicating between themselves quite frequently. You are left out. You are living all alone out here in Europe, so you miss them, but they do not miss each other. You are the one in need so it is only natural that you call. Do not criticize someone for calling only when they need something. That is natural human behavior. You live alone and miss your family so you make the call. Your siblings are all together so they do not feel the need to call you. Also, why would they call you when you always call them first and frequently?

From now on, just call them and finish it with that. Just thank your sister for answering. Don't make the leap to the next thought, "I call you so many times; why do you never call me back?" This logic is inappropriate. If you stop making calls to Korea, then that would end the relationship. That is also natural because your siblings do not feel the need to call you. Make no mistake. Let there be no misunderstanding. You are calling

Monument of the Discoveries

Marquis of Pombal Square

them for your happiness. You go to the mountain because you enjoy going. You demand that the mountain should be responsive. You are so disappointed at the mountain for not giving back, that now you are about to shut yourself out and say, "I will never go to that mountain again, ever!" As a result, you have nowhere to go. That is why you ended up asking me the question. You have created your own prison.

You are a picky investor who wants to see returns. You are not a saint but you try to act as one. That is why suffering arises. If you are really disappointed at your sister, then just tell her you are feeling abandoned because she does not ever call you. Be honest and express yourself.

If you stop calling your sisters, then that does not make you a bad person. Call if you want to call. Do not call if you do not want to call. But I am telling you not to perceive it as a give-and-take. You are engaging in a trade, a psychological trade with your family. Do so if you wish, but you will reap its fruits. If you expect a return, you will start resenting others. Your siblings and their children are not particularly bad people; they are just ordinary people. A mountain is just a mountain. You might like it or dislike it. If you like the mountain, the sea, the flower, then that makes you happy. Stop thinking, "I called you three times. You should at least return one call." That is commerce. Do not create commerce between brothers and sisters. You are insisting, "I have loved you this much. What have you given me in return?" You mistake love for money. Stop the commerce. That is why I always say, "So much for love!" (Laughter.)

Call them if you want. You are the one living abroad, the one who misses your family. It is natural that you call them more often. You would have been very close with your brothers and sisters when you were all young. But when they grew up, got busy with work, got married and had children, it became hard for them to care for their siblings as much. Your sisters have all changed; they are now grannies. On the contrary, your mentality has frozen as a child, at the time you moved to Portugal from Korea twenty-five years ago. You are thinking of the same loving family as it was before you left Korea. Do you realize that? Now, are you or are you not going to call your sisters first?

The woman responded, "I will call her." (Laughter.)

I am extremely restless at home
after my retirement

Ellicott City

An elderly man asked, "I worked for the United States government for thirty-four years. I retired a week ago. Now I stay home all the time. I feel like I have lost all peace. I am uneasy and uncomfortable. I am considering returning to my workplace to start working part-time. Half of me wants to rest; the other half wants to work. What should I do?"

Have you heard of inertia? An object that has been moving wants to keep moving. If it has been stationary, it wants to remain unmoving. To move a fixed object, you need to apply force. To stop a moving object, you also need to spend energy.

You have gone to work every day for the past thirty-four years. Working has become a habit. Suddenly you are out of your job. You feel very strange and uneasy because you are not used to staying home.

How to cure that? If you rest for about one year, it will go away. It has only been one week! Your restlessness will get worse for a month. But after that, it will fade. Play for one year, and you will have developed a new inertia in playing. So do not worry. It just takes time. Time is the healer. Just wait.

If you are a church-goer, go do some volunteering at the church. If you believe in Buddhism, go to the temple to help others. If you find something to do, that also helps soothe your restless soul. But even if you don't do anything, time will still heal you.

Now, whether or not you should go back to work is a completely different question. If you want to keep working, then choose to do so. But do not choose it out of restlessness. If you succumb to your inertia of working, you will die working. The same problem will surface whether you quit at sixty years of age or sixty-five years or at seventy. You have retired once; try to make it an opportunity to break free from your inertia, your karma. Tell yourself you want to become independent and free from habitual propensity. Just rest and play for a year.

After a year's relaxation has dissolved your karma, at that moment, you can reconsider starting work. Decisions made at that state of mind is healthy and autonomous. It does not come from your habit but rather is a mindful and intentional choice that you make. If that is the case, it is good regardless of whether you work or not.

Life is a habit. This habit is called karma. The life of a human is a continuation of this habit. Habit drives and forms you. If you have a smoking habit, you keep wanting to smoke.

Many people are now addicted to smartphones. Machines are handy; you need to use them wisely in order not to become addicted. To prevent it

from becoming a habit, try living without your phone one day in a week, or two days a month. If you feel restless and uneasy, you should realize, "Oh, I have become addicted to my smartphone." To break free from addiction, you need to overcome that restlessness. Only then can you be free. If you have a car, try using public transportation once a month. Do not be attached to the car.

You need to stay away from falling into habits in order to protect yourself. I am not saying you should not use machines at all; I am saying you should be free from them. To you, going to work has become a habit. It has formed over the period of thirty-four years. How can that go away in a week? It will take maybe one year to rid your body and your soul of that habit. If you feel uneasy, tell yourself, "This is because of my habit. But there is nothing wrong. Now is free. Now is good." Keep bringing your mind to peace. If that is not possible, go find some volunteer jobs. Get rid of that karma first, and then after that, if you still want to work, then it is okay to work.

My husband competes with his children

A young woman said, "I am married to an American. I have an issue with him about raising our children. We have two kids. One is three years old; the other is two. I conflict with my husband on how to raise them. My husband is a really nice guy but he has a short temper. In addition, he does not believe in any of the books on childcare. When the children misbehave, he yells at them. He is very tidy, so everything needs to be organized. I feel that the older child is getting hurt from this.

There is nothing wrong between my husband and me. We love each other. My husband did not want children, but I insisted that we should have kids. My husband agreed to this before we got married. But now that we have children, my husband seems to be stressed. He is focused more on our relationship than the parent-child relationship. That stress seems to be directed toward the children. My husband complains more and more. Sometimes he seems to be competing with his children. Should I fight him to raise the kids the way I think is right? Or should I just let my husband have his way? What should I do?"

Your husband did not want any children in the first place. You did not accept his wish at the time of marriage. You did what you wanted and had children. Your husband agreed to have children so that he could marry you. Your husband never wanted children.

This is the source of the problem. Before marriage, all your attention was directed at your husband. Now, it is going to your children. To your husband, they really are competitors. And very strong ones, too. Psychologically it is only natural that he gets frustrated. If your husband is that type of a guy, when you are with him, you should direct all your love only to him. You should give him assurance that the presence of children will not disrupt your love toward him. But you loved your children in a way that made your husband feel left out. In such a setting, emotional conflict is inevitable.

Right away, you must respect your husband's wishes at the time of marriage when he never wanted any children. Your husband agreed to have children because you wanted children. But his subconscious has never changed. His dissatisfaction exists deep in his mind. It is expressed as yelling or complaints. Think and treat him as a child. Think that you are caring for three children. Always tend to the largest child first, and then second and third. Always express attention to your husband. When tending to your children, tell him, "I am sorry, but I will take care of the children for a while." Excuse yourself first and then care for the children.

This can be a very difficult situation between a husband and wife. It is easy for you to think, "This is not just my child; it's yours too!" But if you

want to solve the issue, this is the only way. Your husband did not want children from the beginning. You had your way. You need to give your husband his way. This will reduce his frustration.

When your husband scolds the children, do not intervene. If you step in, this will only increase his anger. Just leave it. If you step in and hug your children, a concept will form in the children's subconscious that, "Mother is good, Father is bad." This will only aggravate the father-child relationship. When your husband reproaches the children, step aside. Pretend you are looking at your neighbor's family. Do not give solace to your children. Instead, pretend it is none of your business.

To raise your children with healthy minds, you need to become wiser. Many infant-rearing books only talk about what a mother should do for the baby but are indifferent to the father. They do not talk about the role of men, even though they are half of the parents! That is why following those books often results in failure. A cow gives birth to a calf, but it never reads any books. Any mother with a healthy body and soul is capable of raising a healthy child.

Embrace your husband. When he frets, coax him. Create and keep a loving relationship. It is vital that you are not stressed if your children are to be healthy. For the children, being scolded by their father is lesser of a trauma than their mother being depressed. It is absolutely crucial that the mother is not in a stressed state when raising her children.

Some families have alcoholic husbands. These men come home and want trouble. But if the wife is perfectly calm and undisturbed, the children will not be negatively influenced. For example, the wife, undisturbed by her husband's being drunk, could casually say, "Oh darling, you are pretty drunk today," instead of starting to argue. Her mind is strong and not affected by her husband's bad behaviors. Father's bad habits are delivered to the child through the mother. If the mother refuses to be a mirror, negativity does not enter the child. About 80 to 90 percent of the child's personality is formed from the mother's influence. If the mother is free from stress, the child will also be comfortable and stable.

Of course, I am not saying that men are allowed to misbehave, and that it is the sole responsibility of women to properly manage the family and raise the children. I do not endorse inappropriate conduct from either sex. Now, I am only talking about how women can respond to misbehaving men because I am answering your question.

So do not just say, "Oh, the father is setting a terrible example for the child." Let's say your child spilled some milk. Your husband may get mad. Do not confront your husband, "He is only a child! He can spill milk." It is wiser to tell your husband, "Darling, it was an accident. I should have put the milk away." This is to sooth the husband. Do not start criticizing your husband. He will only get more stressed. Of course, this is not easy for any woman. But remember that you chose a man who never wanted a child. You should not have married him or you should not have had any children. Have it your way and there is a price you pay. If you deem your husband to be the source of the problem and make up your mind to "fix" him, this means that ultimately you want to have everything your way. If you two are loving, you are the one that must understand and tolerate your husband's tendencies. If you can do that, there will be a minimal negative influence on your children.

I want to have a purpose,
a dream

/

Kansas City

/

A lady asked, "I am in my forties. I raised two children. They've grown up and started college two or three years ago. That was when I started to feel restless. I have more time than before, but I am not happy. I kept thinking, 'Why am I not happy?' I found that I was living without a purpose or a dream. I am already over forty. How can I handle this wisely so that I may live the rest of my life for a dream?"

There are three ways. First is a crisis falling on you. If a crisis comes, your problems will go. For instance, if your husband dies, or if you lose your job, or if your child gets sick, or if you get cancer or something, you will never think of such problems. Then you should realize that the crisis is actually a blessing. But would you be wise enough to realize that, "Oh, it is because this crisis has come that I could solve my problem and get over my unhappy feeling"? That means if there were God who listened to your prayer, God would give you a disaster. Because the crisis, despite the hardship it brings, will solve your issue of that unhappy feeling.

Second, if God did not gift you with a crisis, you would keep on living with that issue. You are currently physically comfortable but mentally ever restless. A catastrophe would give physical hardship but solve your mental problem. Which one would you prefer? At least from this perspective, is not the present better? Of course, you would desire neither.

Third, there is a way other than these two. You should start by praying to God that you are thankful for being alive. "Thank you, Lord. In your blessing, I am alive." You have eaten well, your husband is working, your kids are healthy. Thanking should come first. If you are thankful, how do you pay that back? You received a blessing; how do you give back to the Lord? But the Lord is too great. The Lord does not need anything. What did God say? "Whatsoever you do to the least of my people, that you do unto me." God had said that if you want to do something for God, do instead, five things for the most destitute of the people. Give water to the thirsty, food to the hungry, clothes to the naked, medicine to the sick, care for the refugees or prisoners. This is how you repay for the blessings you have received. If you do that, your happiness persists. Because this kind of happiness is like a spring that never dries. Take the water out, and the water will seep back in.

If you want to live a happy life, I suggest you don't try to make more money but instead do some volunteering. You can cook food, clean, give food to the homeless, and explore many more options. Energy will spring out of your heart and you will be happy. You will be content with your life. You will argue much less with your family. You will feel more thankful for your husband and children.

Which will you choose? Would you walk the third path of giving back for the blessing you have received? Do you prefer to suffer from a tragedy so that your mind will no longer be occupied with thoughts? Do you want to keep walking the path of unhappy thoughts that leads you to depression? Which way will you go?

The lady asked again, "I had reached a conclusion that I shall get a job in order to be satisfied with myself. How can I find a job that makes me happy?"

That is the road to disaster. You are inviting tragedy. You seek self-satisfaction. That is greed. What I am telling you is that, for example, if you volunteer for others, you will develop a sense of self-respect, humbleness, and pride. On the contrary, if you seek to please yourself, you will never get it. You do not understand what I am saying. Do not think that getting a job and making some money will bring you self-respect. You seem to feel that being a housewife is somewhat inferior. Do not think like that. Being a housewife is actually privileged in that they can go out to do volunteering. This could be a blessing from God. Your husband is making money so you do not have to worry about that. Use your talent for some other good. Do not sell it away at a cheap price. Use it for a better purpose. Of course, if your husband loses his job, you can use your talent for your family.

One who gives money is the master. One who receives is the servant.

"I am alive due to your Grace."

Pray and remember to be grateful for being alive, for having food for the day.
Your spouse is working hard,
children are healthy.
Be grateful for all these.
Every morning, open your eyes and pray as such.

You are blessed to be a master; why do you want to become a slave? Many of the people here want to be masters but cannot because they must make a living. They have no choice but to be slaves. When the conditions are set, you can start returning all the blessings back to the society. Then the blessing will continue to come. If you continue to think like you do now, in a self-centered way, blessing will just bounce off.

If you are wise, you will start following the teachings of the Saints even before you fully understand them. Your level of wisdom might not be able to grasp them, however, have faith in the path suggested by the Saints; and start practicing the merits. You have heard the words of wisdom. So, when you go back home, first, take out a few thousand dollars or any amount and give it to the poor. Second, do not pray for your wishes but offer prayers of gratitude. Third, do volunteer works to pay back for the blessings you enjoy. This will immediately rid you of gloomy thoughts. Then the dream you are looking for will appear. Volunteer for at least three years. Then a path will appear. If you really want to get a job, get one at that state. If you start working after reaching that mental state, your mind will be different, much more comfortable. However, if you get a job now, you might enjoy it at first but later it will come back as a disaster. Have knowledge of such principles and prepare in advance. Then you will live a happier life.

How can I love myself?

Philadelphia

A man asked, "I am never satisfied. It has been such a long time since I last felt happiness. I do not give to others. I do not know how to love. I want to know how to love myself. How can I discard my desires and become satisfied?"

You said you suffer because you can neither give nor love. I am afraid that is not true. Look at the rabbit in the mountains. Does that rabbit know how to give? How to love? No. A rabbit does neither, but it does not suffer from that, never. Nothing is wrong. You might not be able to give, to love, but that is not the problem. You cannot say you suffer because of that.

The audience here, most of the people here, they think only of themselves. They just live on like that. But still, they have no trouble. Chipmunks don't care for others. But a chipmunk lives on, lives well. You are the one who is serious about your problem, but you have created it. The problem is problematized by you but in reality it is not a problem. There is

"I am never satisfied. It has been such a long time since I last felt happiness."

"Could it be that you desire too much?

Why not live like a rabbit?

Look how satisfied it is all the time."

no problem; there is no need for suffering.

Wanting to become the president or a millionaire is not greed. What is greed? It is not a matter of how big or small the desire is. Greed is when a contradiction exists. You borrowed money, but you don't want to pay back. You never saved money, but you want to spend money. This contradicting desire is greed. Logically, this cannot happen, but with your mind wish it so. This is greed. More precisely, it is ignorance. The source of suffering is ignorance. Greed belongs to ignorance. Anger is also a part of ignorance.

The cause of suffering is ignorance, but there are three detailed categories. First is greed. Greed is the desire to have everything as you want. Second is the anger arising from the belief that you are right. Third is foolishness or ignorance. These are the three toxins that poison our minds. Greed is different from intention. The intention is the will to do something, and you can get it done. Greed, on the other hand, can never be accomplished. Greed always invites suffering. That is why Buddhism teaches you to let go of your greed.

As for you, I do not think you are being greedy. You know only how to receive love but know not how to give. That is not greed.

Then what is your greed? Think about that.

Look at the chipmunk. A chipmunk cannot climb all trees. It cannot cross all creeks. But have you ever seen a chipmunk grieving over such reality? You are better than a chipmunk, right? A chipmunk never self-tortures. Why should you? Do not suffer. If you suffer, it means you are more ignorant than the chipmunk. Suffering normally arises when you are greedy or angry. That is what you have to observe in you.

You seem to be tightly bound by the thought that you have to love and give. You are being greedy about giving love. If you can love, love. If you can give, give. Don't force them upon yourself. Do not think that you must love or must give. You are trying to give more than you can. That is why you are unsatisfied. Live like the rabbits. How relaxed they are!

My husband is addicted to gambling.

Las Vegas

An elderly lady asked, "My husband and I previously lived in San Jose and it's been a year since we moved to Las Vegas. My husband goes to play poker five times a week. I tell him not to go but he would never listen to me. Whenever he goes to gamble, I become severely depressed. I try to watch your YouTube talks to overcome my depression but I cannot.

I followed my husband to the casino a few times. I saw these addicted people playing games. I totally despise them. Their eyes are not normal. I believe my husband still has sanity in his eyes, but I just hate the thought of him being in that insane crowd. We came here after retirement because we thought it could be entertaining here. Of course, I agreed to move here. Before we moved, he promised that he would not play poker."

It is in the human nature to make and break promises. Look at yourself. You promise yourself that you will not nag your husband again, but you break your promise all the time. It is the same with him. Your husband gave his word, but every night, when darkness falls, he is swept away by

218

this craving to gamble. What can he do? That is what addiction is about. He did not lie to you. At the time of that promise, he really was going to stay away from poker. But when he sees it, sees the ads, thinks of it, he gets this irresistible urge.

When your husband goes out, tell him, "It breaks my heart that you are going there." Simply and plainly express what you feel. But do not say, "Do not go there because it is breaking my heart." This is different. This is asking the other person to be responsible for causing you pain. That is unpleasant for your husband to hear. But you can't just say nothing. So simply and plainly tell him how you feel, but don't blame him.

How is your living? Do you have a house? Are you doing well financially?

"Yes. He does not gamble to the extent that he loses all he has."

So he has some self-control. Then just trust him. You always break your promise not to nag. It is the same.

"How can my nagging and his gambling be the same?"

Why are they not? They are all habits. Playing poker is a habit, children playing computer games is a habit, checking cellphones every morning is a habit, drinking coffee is a habit, smoking is a habit, taking drugs is a habit, nagging is a habit, getting angry is a habit. How can you say that your habit is a hobby and someone else's habit is an addiction? That is like saying that if you love, it is a romance; if others love, that is an affair. (Laughter.)

"But I believe there are good habits and bad habits. Poker is definitely a very bad one."

No. You have a worse habit. Nagging, getting angry and frustrated, these are some very bad habits. Actually, they are the worst.

"Are you saying that I should just watch and do nothing when my husband goes to play poker?"

I am not telling you to leave him alone whatever he does. I am saying that if you and he have different ideas, you can say, "Darling, this is how I think. I'd prefer you not do that." This is expressing your view. However, you are convinced that your husband is a bad person because he plays poker. That is not good. You are free to express your opinion which is that you do not want him to play poker. He is free to accept that or not. Don't be a dictator.

We live in a democracy. Stop thinking like a dictator. If something makes you mad, tell him that the action makes you mad, not that he himself makes you mad. You are the one who generates madness, not another person. Getting mad is a habit. Just as it is hard for you to quit nagging, it is the same for your husband. Understand and accept that.

Heading to Las Vegas past the wind power plants in the desert of California.

Once you accept your husband, then you can change your own habit. Because you did not understand your husband, you could not stop nagging. But if you understand and accept, you will nag no more, your habits will change, and conversations will become much smoother.

"I fully understand what you are saying. But can't you just tell my husband to quit gambling?" (Laughter.)

Why would I meddle in your husband's life? He wouldn't listen to me anyway. If you want your husband to listen to you, change your demands. Say, "Honey, please go to gamble more than five times a week." (Laughter.) Try this. Then you will have the most compliant husband in the world. There are many ways to make your husband listen to you, but you insist on ways that make him not listen.

"What is the difference between right and wrong to you? From a common sense perspective, I believe playing poker belongs to something bad."

It is legal to gamble in Las Vegas. It is perfectly okay; the law says so. (Laughter.) How would the people of Las Vegas survive if everyone opposed gambling like you do? People come from all over the world to this desert to gamble. The more people from afar come and lose money here, the better the economy here gets. (Laughter.) I asked why the economy wasn't doing so good in this area and they told me that all the gamblers went to Macau.

If more people think like you, it will be a disaster for Las Vegas. The economy will collapse. More states are legalizing gambling so fewer people are coming here. Restaurants and other retail businesses are not doing well. I went to a restaurant earlier. The owner told me that business was bad because fewer people visited. So I said, "That is a good thing. If fewer people gamble, is that not a better world?" (Laughter.)

You see, there is no right or wrong, good or bad. If smoking is banned, it becomes a bad thing. If it is legal, it is regarded as a hobby. If marijuana is prohibited, it is looked upon as evil. If allowed, it becomes a leisure activity. Same with poker. It is acceptable if allowed but becomes a crime if the law determines so.

There is no such thing as inherently good or evil. These concepts are in our society's making. What the society instructs, we comply with. Here, the society has made gambling legal. In this situation, do not fight too much over whether gambling is good or bad.

The wife replied, "Okay then. I will tell him to go gambling every day."
(Laughter.)

No. No. You don't need to choose the other extreme. There is no need to tell him to go gamble every day, nor is there a need to tell him to stop gambling. Just let him live his life. Just let yourself express your views when you are unhappy. There is nothing wrong with being honest with your feelings to your husband. Tell him your opinion anytime you want, but do not give out orders. Think of it. It would be terribly unpleasant for your husband to hear you talking like a boss. Stop trying to control him. Just be grateful that he is living with you! (Laughter.)

People discriminate against me
for not eating meat

Mexico City

A woman asked, "I want to ask you about eating. I stopped eating meat in 2009. I eat fish though. I was a vegetarian for over five years. I find that people are constantly attacking me about my eating habits. When I finally get to the point of explaining to them the reason why I quit eating meat, they are not even interested! They just say, 'Why do you think you are so special? Just eat meat.' How can I convince these people wisely without quarreling?"

Don't do anything. Just eat what you like. I think those people are not attacking you but are feeling curious and interested. When a Korean Buddhist monk eats meat, people will be curious and interested. That is because monks are not allowed to eat meat. That is the idea people have. Conversely, people have the idea that ordinary people do eat meat. That is why they are curious when they see a vegetarian. Don't accept it as an attack; it's just their curiosity.

You can be a vegetarian for your health, for the environment, for love of life. You might be horrified by the abject conditions in which livestock animals live and are butchered. All such attitudes are good; they come from kindness and compassion.

First, people eat too much meat nowadays. It is good for your health to cut down on meat.

Second, an excessive meat diet has triggered a food crisis on our planet. If you compare eating one kilogram (2.2 pounds) of grain to eating one kilogram of meat, the latter requires much more resources. A cow or a pig needs to eat 5 kg (11 lb.) of grain to put on 1 kg of meat. That means if you consume 1 kg of meat, you are consuming 5 kg of grains. That is an excessive consumption of food resources. The market will try to meet the demand. Farmers increase their production. This, in turn, calls for a heavier use of chemical fertilizers. Nowadays corporations are even turning to genetically-modified beans and corn. The problem is getting worse and worse. A vegetarian diet can be a significant movement in addressing the environmental and food crises.

Third, in the past, chickens, pigs, and other animals had a relatively good life before they were butchered. However, in the modern era, animals live in the most horrible of conditions in intensive growing facilities. These animals suffer enormously. They easily fall ill due to stress, prompting farmers to use a lot of antibiotics. To make ends meet, they inject growth hormones to make animals fatter faster. In a natural state, it takes six months for a chicken to mature, but for hens on farms it only takes 38 days. This is the root cause behind avian influenza, swine influenza, and mad cow disease. It is highly possible that more and more mutated forms of viruses will occur. Also, food has an influence on the human personality. Toxicity in the meat can have a negative impact on our minds.

Rather than telling people to quit eating meat, it is better to suggest a reduction in meat consumption considering these problems. If you say you do not eat meat, people tend to be cynical. "Don't tell me what to do." "How much longer do you think you can live?" "Do you think you will get much prettier?" "You are not going to save the Earth." If you present eating meat as evil, people who eat meat, you see, would naturally want to defend their actions and/or criticize you.

So soften your words and attitude. "Too much meat can raise cholesterol levels. It is better for your health to cut down on meat. If you want meat, try eating fish. What is tasty to the tongue is not necessarily good for the body. I decided to cut down on meat a bit." This kind of wording will invite fewer attacks. If the other person offers you meat, politely say that you had too much meat before. If after a few conversations, you feel that the person is ready for such talks, you can explain the benefits of a vegetarian diet. Don't talk too much, for the people will think you are bumptious. Simply mention one or two points regarding health or environment.

The lady added, "People eat a lot of meat here in Mexico. They eat meat like Koreans eat rice. A side-effect I am experiencing is that after quitting meat, I eat lots of bread and other snacks. When I am stressed out at work,

I eat chocolates or sweets. I tend to over-eat. How can I control this?"

A true practitioner would change the habit of eating, not just substitute meat for another food. If you change from opium to marijuana, or from marijuana to cocaine or to cigarettes, that is not good. You should observe your own eating habits. Whenever desire arises, you should practice how not to succumb to it.

As much as you are able to control your desire for meat, you should be able to do that for all other foods. That is the way to liberalization. If you substitute one desire for another, that is not the way of a practitioner. Do not just refrain from meat but also foster the will-power to control your desire for all food. Do not suppress your desires, because suppressing means there is something to suppress. Of course, in the beginning, you do need to suppress your desires sometimes, but gradually you will reach a stage where there is nothing to suppress. Try to reach the level where you are liberated from food. If you speak from that level, people will listen more.

"Thank you. Is there any other advice for people with eating disorders?"

Attachment to food such as binging is a response to stress. Some people smoke, eat junk food, buy tons of shoes or clothes to reduce stress. Stress is what needs to be addressed, and it should be addressed through practice. It is meaningless to leave the stress alone and just change the object of your indulgence. Binge eating is just one of the many symptoms of stress.

Lost

Life does not carry an ultimate purpose. We just eat and live, live and eat.

Do not think so grandiosely of your life. Live light-heartedly, live light.

You load yourself with heavy burdens and lament that you cannot fly.

I have no purpose in life

/

Manhattan

/

A young woman said, "I am in my early forties. I have a job. Since I was little, I have always had goals. I wanted to go to university. I wanted a good job. When I got a job, I prepared for various certifications. I was quite successful in my career, so I thought I should be happy. But from my mid-thirties on, I began to have doubts. I thought, 'Why have I lived like this, so busy, so mindless?' So I quit my job three years ago and went to Japan. I enjoyed, relaxed, and played as much as I wanted for two years. Now, I have come back to the United States and have another job that is less stressful, but it also comes with a lower salary. My mind is quite peaceful, but a part of me started asking, 'Is it okay to live a purposeless life like this?' I am not sure what a good life is."

What is a good life? A life where you do not think about good life. A life with no worries. But if you desire to live like you did in the past, where you were busy like crazy, then go back to doing it. You voluntarily let go of that lifestyle because you thought that was not quite right. Now that you ask me whether your choice was right, I am telling you that it was not wrong. Nothing is wrong. For the planet, for the States, for you as an individual, your choice is not a problem.

The lady asked, "Then why do I feel empty?"

It is because of your habit. Your addiction to busy life has not yet been completely removed. Your habit remains in your subconscious. Because of that, when you want to rest, a deep part of you resists. It starts thinking that you are wasting time. For example, if someone is addicted to tobacco or alcohol, that person will crave them. They want to have the best quality cigarettes or liquor. However, no matter how high-quality they are, they still harm you. It is best not to indulge in them. So the path you should take is obvious. Break free from addiction. You must realize that the best way is not to take them at all.

What you see in the world is people seeking better and better quality cigarettes and liquors. You need not think, "Am I being left out? Am I losing in the competition?" If those thoughts arise, it means your old habits still remain. For a non-smoker or non-drinker, what use is top-quality tobacco or whiskey? There might be people who have all the money in the world, but if you do not believe in the importance of money, there is nothing to envy or worry. All the people in the world might be rushing in the same direction, but if the end is a cliff, there is no reason that you should follow them. You still hold on to tendencies from your past.

Karma follows the rule of inertia. We continue what we have continued. You have a habit from the past, so even though you try to tell yourself, "That is not good. I will break away from it," your subconscious does not accept that. Play some more, and you will get better. (Laughter.)

"I feel that it was greed that drove my life in the past, and now I live without any thought or aim."

Living without any thought is good, but you must not become lazy or lethargic. If you have a lot of time, then do some volunteering. I have heard there are many people in New York who are hungry. Join a charity or social organization that provides food for them. Look around – there are so many things you can do. You need not sit around thinking about the emptiness of your life. You can meditate, practice yoga, or volunteer. There are always things to do.

What is greed? If you say, "I want to become a millionaire," that is not greed. Greed is when you set a goal, but do not make the effort needed to accomplish it. You want good grades, but you do not study. You want money, but you do not work. That is greed. You want something you do not deserve. Setting a goal and working towards it is not greed. There is a simple criterion you can use to tell whether something is greed or not. If you fail to accomplish the goal and you despair, that is greed. But if you fail and are not discouraged, but rather continue your pursuit in different ways, that is not greed. You keep studying, analyzing, developing new approaches; then no matter how big your goal is, it will not be defined as greed.

Why do you get stressed? It is because of greed. Why do students get stressed? Because they want grades better than they deserve. Why do employees get stressed? Because they want to be recognized as more capable than they really are. Just be you. I am not saying you should give only half of what you have got. Do your best, but do not worry about the results. There is a proverb, "Humans do the work; heaven accomplishes." This does not mean that heaven is the ultimate determining force. It is to teach you that you should do your best and not worry about the outcome. What else is there to do after you have done your best? Nothing! Your life can then become comfortable and happy.

"So you are telling me that it is okay to keep working in this job, without any major purpose?"

Do you think a chipmunk has a purpose in life? Ask the chipmunk. Life does not carry an ultimate purpose. We just eat and live, live and eat. But if you have some extra time, you can do some good for others. Do not think so grandiosely of your life. When you do that, your life can become less happy than an animal's. Humans have degraded the meaning of life so much with their own hands that now people envy a bird, a bird soaring through the sky. Life has become too much of a suffering. You load yourself with heavy burdens and lament that you cannot fly.

Live light-heartedly, live light. If you have money, give to others. If you have time, work for others. Engage with the society; then, you will naturally find a purpose, find a good use for your talents. Your purpose thus far has been to make money and succeed; but that can change. So you need not worry now. You are in the process of being cleansed from your past. You will have some more confusion and worry, but that is fine. Live on. You will find relaxation and peace. Do some work for others, give money to the poor. You will be happy and so will others.

I changed my sex

Tacoma

A person asked, "I had lived as a man for over forty years. It was not fun anymore. It has been a year since I started changing my life into a third sex. This life is so much more fun; I am enjoying every moment of it. I am worried whether I should tell my parents. My parents are in their mid-70s and both are healthy. They are strict and conservative. I am not sure if they can take the shock. I visit Korea once or twice a year. Whenever I visit, I used to go to the public spa with my father. I am in a difficult situation now. I am not sure whether I should hide this from them or tell them frankly. If I tell them, how should I do it?"

Is your situation natural or induced by hormones?

The person replied, "Since I was little, I have wondered whether or not I am a girl. Since puberty, I felt that my mind and my body did not match. However, I managed to get along without any big problems. I was a soccer player and a swimmer. I even completed military service. I divorced three

years ago. Now that I do not have to worry about others, I wanted to do
something that I had dreamt of for a long time. I had been married for
about thirteen years. We did not have children but still had sexual inter-
course. People usually think that it is the homosexuals who change sexes but
in fact, I am bisexual. I heard that bisexuals are very rare. However, I want
to live as a woman. How can I tell my parents?"

Why not live with the mind of a woman? How your body looks is not
so important. Why not just keep your body? You can forget about whether
your body looks like a man or a woman.

The questioner explained, "If I take hormones, it affects my emotions.
Things that happen to me are not something people born as men or women
can understand."

So, you are taking hormones to develop female traits in your body.
That is your freedom, but it is still against nature. For example, if you are
born with a man's body but are not sexually interested in women, then it
makes sense to recognize homosexuality because you can do nothing about
it. Something you are born with is not your responsibility. But you were
born with a man's body and are bisexual. You are intentionally turning
your body into a woman's with hormones. You are free to do that but do
you really have to?

"It has already begun, and I can't go back. I have no desire to stop."

If you removed your penis, why not dress up as a man when you meet your parents if you do not want to shock them? I think it is better to tell your parents on matters that are given, things that you cannot change. If you were born with something, I think it is right to tell them. They may be shocked, but it was something you could do nothing about. It was not that you did something against your parents' will. It was a given condition. However, on matters that you made a choice on, learning of them may cause too extreme a shock for your parents. It might be better to keep it a secret. Disguise as a man when meeting your parents. Maybe that is better. You don't need to shock your elderly parents. Of course, however, it is ultimately your decision.

If you can have what you want and make your parents happy at the same time, that is the best. However, a change in their son's sex could be too hard for your parents to accept. Is telling your parents such an urgent matter? You can just say you are too busy with work in the States that you do not have time to see them. Live as a woman here and dress as a man when you go to Korea and be a good son. It could be wiser to keep it secret from them. I think the shock of this would be even greater than that of their child becoming a monk, nun or a priest.

Life, ultimately, is a choice you make. If you are not harming others, people should not judge whether that is right or wrong. There are four basic ethics. One, do not kill others so I may live. Two, do not harm others so

I may profit. Three, do not give pain to others so I may enjoy. Four, do not slander or scam others so I may benefit. These four are the most important. Apart from these, don't intervene in other people's lives, and don't let others judge and dictate your own life. Live as you will. The choice is for you to make. But if you choose against the law of nature, there can be side effects.

You want to change the natural order because of your preference. That is okay but if your happiness causes suffering and shock to your parents, think twice before telling them. Especially since the sex-change was your own choice, not something you could not avoid, I believe it is wiser to keep your parents from the shock.

I have lied and deeply hurt my husband

Taipei

A young lady asked, "My husband absolutely detests lying. Before marriage, we both promised that we would never lie to one another. But after marriage, I was the one who broke that promise. My husband was extremely disappointed and angry. It took a long time to recover but finally we did reconcile. I promised again that I would not lie. However, it must have traumatized my husband, as he keeps talking about the past. We promised to forget about that incident but it seems that my husband cannot do that. He is constantly bringing it up, I now feel sorry, uncomfortable, and angry at the same time. How can my husband be healed?"

When you are sexually abused as a small girl and it leaves a permanent nightmare, we call it trauma. Trauma will not go away; it will be with you your whole life. You can get help from psychiatrists or psychoanalysts. But it is not easy to heal. It is the same in your body. A serious injury leaves a scar. Your husband has a scar in his heart. That scar is more sensitive than other parts, it hurts to the touch, it sometimes erupts again.

Women who have had the unfortunate experience of sexual abuse find it extremely hard to overcome it. If they do not heal completely through psychotherapy or other means, they will have trouble in managing relations with men. Even if she loves a guy or gets married, when she makes love, if some action reminds her of the experience of being raped, she will suddenly be enraged or fearful. Consequently, the man will find it difficult to understand such a woman. One moment they were hugging and the next moment she is overwhelmed with rage. Such a relationship is hard to manage. On the woman's body, there are no traces of violence. The scar persists in her mind. That is why treatment is necessary.

In the past, people were ignorant about healing an injury to the mind. When soldiers returned from Vietnam, society cared only for their bodies. They were ignorant of the need to heal the minds. However, many veterans found it impossible to adapt to society due to their mental trauma; some of them would commit crimes or suicide. Now we have a term for this, "post-traumatic stress disorder" or PTSD.

Korean society is the same. There are around 30,000 North Koreans who escaped their country and came to South Korea. The South Korean government provides economic assistance such as introducing jobs, supporting housing, and so forth, but is ignorant about providing them with psychological assistance. Why do you think these North Koreans fail to adapt to South Korean society? They worked in North Korea for less than a dollar a day; in China, they earned 5 dollars a day; in Korea, they can

make 50 dollars a day. Yet, what could be wrong?

It is because they have been traumatized. This trauma makes it impossible for them to adapt. South Koreans find it difficult to understand because they have no idea about the trauma in the North Koreans' hearts. It is not a simple difference in cultures. It is more than that. The scars in these people keep getting re-infected again and again.

For example, a North Korean joined a soccer club. A member asked him whether there were any soccer balls in North Korea. The member asked without any intentions, out of pure curiosity, or even probably good will, trying to start a conversation. You can be curious because you heard that people starve to death in North Korea. However, this North Korean erupted into anger and assaulted the questioner. The police had to come to the scene to take them away. What do you think? This violent reaction was caused by mental scars. "Do I look so funny to you? Do you seriously think we don't even have a soccer ball?" This person would have suppressed himself a lot through the many experiences of discrimination he encountered in the south. These are mental scars. Fortunately, nowadays more people realize that mental therapy is crucial. Actually, mental healing is much more important than physical treatment.

You must understand that your husband has been traumatized. He has never overcome his shock. His scar is not healed. You apologized and he accepted. But sooner or later, it surfaces to his consciousness again. He can't stop it from rising, stop thinking of it. You must repent for the rest of your life.

The young woman said "I am in my twenties. Are you serious about having to repent for the rest of my life?"

Whenever your husband brings it up, always say, "I am sorry." Do it again and again and again. Only that will stop his scar from erupting. Say, "I am sorry from the bottom of my heart." That will likely alleviate his obsession. Do not say, "What do you want me to do? How many times do we have to go over this? I apologized over and over." This will only aggravate his scar; the argument will not stop.

This mindset is actually common in all assailants. Those who did the damage think that giving apology was enough. But the victim feels that the guilty person is only apologizing 10 percent, when the apology should be 100 percent. So victims always say, "That apology was not genuine." Then it is the assailant's turn to get mad. This gives further excuse to the victim to criticize the assailant for an insincere apology. So I suggest that every time your husband brings up the issue, you apologize sincerely. Do it again and again. Then the problem will not get worse. Do not say, "Do I have to talk about that again?" If you go this way, it is better to get a divorce.

"What happens if I continue to apologize?"

Do not think that you are apologizing. Don't take it too heavily. When he brings up the issue, don't strike back. Just say, "I am sorry. I really am."

Just say it even if you do not feel like it 100 percent. He is your husband. If you understand him, his trauma, you should be able to do this in the least.

You are the one who committed a serious wrong. Don't try to settle this so easily with one apology. You want a one-time event to clear everything and heal the trauma; it doesn't work that way. In his head, the memory is vivid like a video. It constantly comes back, rises linked to other things, and he is reminded every so often. Then as a wife, you should think, "Oh, how deep he has been hurt!" and embrace. Every time the scar opens and bleeds again, you should fathom the depth of his scar, feel really sorry. Think again of how deeply your husband was hurt. Then without hesitation, you will say, "I am sorry." But you do not seem to be thinking as such. You seem to be thinking, "You can lie once in a while. Stop blaming me. How can a person keep all the promises?" Can you tell me what it is that you lied about?

"I spent some money but lied and said that I didn't."

Tell your husband that you really had to urgently use the money but after that, you didn't have the courage to tell him the truth. Tell him that over and over. You have planted a seed of doubt in your husband and he will not trust you for life. That is how it is.

For you, that incident was not such a serious thing. You are thinking that promises can be broken in some situations. Indeed, you tried to keep your promise and it was the first time you broke it. However, for your husband, that would not have been the first time he had been let down by a promise. I suspect that he would have been traumatized, in his youth or some time which he may not even remember, by his parents or someone whom he deeply trusted lying to him. Such an experience has made him susceptible to shock from a close person lying. That is his karma. He made a promise with you to avoid such suffering before marriage. Now, despite his efforts, despite his trust in you, he experienced betrayal once again. This time, it is his wife. He is crying out to you, "How could you?" His trust in you has been broken.

You must understand that your husband is particularly sensitive to this issue. Again, just say, "I am sorry." An ordinary person might tolerate ten lies. Because after a few experiences, the person can realize that someone is lying and thinks, "I will only trust half of what he says." That is the flexibility we have. But your husband is different. Because of that trauma, he will react differently. Just one lie and he is in shock. This is not such a big issue once you understand him. It can be trivial for you, but for your husband it is tremendous. Always remember that. That is why you should keep saying, "I am sorry" whenever the issue is brought up.

How can I become
a good father, a good husband?

A middle-aged man asked, "I have been married for eight years. I have a seven-year-old son and a five-year-old daughter. How can I be a better father, husband, and make my family happier? My wife and kids are in Ho Chi Minh. I live alone in Hanoi. Sometimes I feel hollow inside; I think that has to do with my living alone. I know I am making a sacrifice for my family but why do I feel empty?"

You feel empty because you think you are making a sacrifice for your family. Such thoughts will only stress you. "I am doing this for my family, my kids, my wife, etc." This is a sense of duty. If you have duty on your shoulders, they are heavy. Your face cannot be bright with such a burden. Discard the thought of "Doing it for somebody." Think with a cool head. Do you like to live alone or with your wife? Which do you prefer?

"It would be good to live together."

My question was not if it is good to be together. Do you prefer to live alone not having married, or do you prefer to be married whether you are together or not?

The man replied, "I believe that a man and a woman have to marry unless they want to devote themselves to religion."

Your answer is too complicated. Is it better for you to be married? Is it better to be alone? Just say yes or no.

"In my position, I think getting married is better."

Do you prefer to live with your wife without kids? Or do you want to have two kids even though you need to work harder?

"My case is the latter. That is my dilemma."

Which makes you happier? To live with a wife without kids or to have kids? What made you happier – kids or no kids?

"I have kids, so currently it is better with kids."

You have a very indirect way of answering things. If you live with a sense of duty such as, "I will do this for my wife, do that for my kids," your life will be unhappy. Don't try to sacrifice everything; you are not a saint. You must be honest, particularly with yourself.

You said you prefer to be with a wife rather than not; to be with kids rather than not. If the overall score is just 51 out of 100, that is better for you. You are living with your wife for your good, not for your wife's. You are raising your children for your good, not for your children's.

Things are not perfect. There will be stress from having a family. But always think, "I am happy because I have you." Don't try to sacrifice for your wife or kids. Always tell your kids, "Thank you. I am happy because of you." Tell your wife, "You nag me sometimes, but still, you make my life happy." Such thoughts will make you a better husband and father. Do not think, "What should I do for my wife, my kids?" Action based on sacrifice is unsustainable.

There is a limit to patience. Normally three is the maximum. Then people run out of patience. If you sacrifice yourself, people might praise you, but you yourself cannot persist. You will start having regrets. "Why should I live like this? Why should I sacrifice myself? Why should I be enslaved to my family?" This makes your life unsustainable. Regrets will eventually make you angry or quit.

Never ask the question, "What should I do for my wife, for my kids?" This question can turn toxic. Just live for your own happiness. What do you think?

"I want myself and all my colleagues, working hard in this foreign coun-

일시 : 8월 26일(화)~12월 18일(목) / 유럽, 러시아, 북미, 중남미, 오세아니아, 아시아
주최 : 정토회 / 주관 : 정토회 해외지부 & 지역정토

try, to work harder for their families."

What do you mean? I told you not to work harder for your family. Your thoughts have not changed. Do not work for others. Doing such will make you want something in return. Such as, "I am doing this much for you. Is that all you can give me in return?" If these negative emotions persist, you start lamenting. Stop living for others; you will be stressed. If mom and dad are fighting every day, putting pressure and wanting something from their children in return for their love, even if they have a lot of money and provide their children with an expensive education, the children will still go wrong.

But if the parents are happy together, the children will naturally be fine. Because showing the love between a mother and a father is the most important role that parents have to play. Then the children will grow up fine even if their grades are a bit low. So it is foolish for mom and dad to argue because of their children. Just be loving. A loving husband is the best father. A caring wife is the best mother. Simple as that. Tell yourself, "I am happy because I have a wife. I am fortunate because I can see her once a month." That makes you realize how precious your wife is. Now, that you are married, it is best for you to live together. If you cannot, you need to discuss making arrangements on how to be together. Of course, being together would be best.

For example, if your income is 3,000 dollars living together with your family in Ho Chi Minh, and is 5,000 dollars living here alone, it is much better to lose 2,000 dollars and live with your family. I know there is a prestigious international school in Ho Chi Minh City and Hanoi doesn't have one. But sending kids to a good school in Ho Chi Minh where they have to live without their father is not worth it. I would recommend sending them to an ordinary school where their parents can be together. Showing them how loving and happy their mom and dad are is the best education.

Do not make a sacrifice for your children. If you sacrifice, your children will go wrong. Because any parent that makes a sacrifice will want something in return from their children. This will be a burden to the kids; they will be uncomfortable. They will try to please their parents all the time. If a boy grows up under such parents, he will likely become a mama's boy. Even when he grows up and gets married, he will not be independent.

So a parent's role is to free their children, free them from any burden. Let them be completely free. "Go and live as you will. The world is yours. You may live alone, get married, marry a black person or a white person or a disabled person. Do everything and anything as you will, as you wish, I support you completely." You should let your children go out into the wild so that they grow strong and tough. Don't treat them like puppies on your leash. You are tugging at the leash all the time. "That is not the way to go. No, go this way. Stop and turn." You are turning your children into puppies.

You say you do it for your children but you are, in fact, projecting your desire upon your children. You are materializing your desire through your children. That is not right. If mother and father live separately, and they say that that sacrifice is for their children, that is a lie. Don't do that. If you have married, live together, be strong. If parenting children is too difficult for you, your children are likely to go wrong. Children giving hardship to their parents cannot grow up to be good people. If parents keep telling their baby, "We are so happy because of you," the baby will definitely grow up fine. That child is already making the parents happy.

I understand that raising kids is difficult, but always try to be positive, be happy, be grateful. Do not think of it as a burden. Some parents even think, "If only it weren't for those kids..." They do not have a clear view, a right thought. They do not have wisdom. And if by some accident their children die, they weep as if the world came to an end. Why live such a regretful life?

Why do I need to get married?

A young lady asked, "I turned thirty recently. I am thinking a lot about marriage. My parents especially have an urgency to get me married. But if I look around, the divorce rate is over fifty percent. If marriage is a failed system, why should I enter one? I once loved a man, but we eventually broke up. I get scared when I think that after living together until old age, one day my husband and I might separate. What attitude should I have toward marriage? How should I determine whom to marry?"

Why do you ask a monk? (Laughter.) You see, there are no musts or must-nots. There is no such thing as "you must marry" or "must not marry." In the past, society was such that everybody got married. That was the culture. They all accepted the marriage system as natural. Your parents belong to that generation. That is why they cannot imagine their children over thirty years of age without a spouse. So you understand that is the way your parents think. Now, it is up to you to accept their views or not.

Again, nothing is right or wrong; there is no one right answer.

You think too much about marriage, and that is why you cannot get married. You make things too complicated. Marriage is a simple thing: it is a man and a woman living together. Don't even worry about the wedding ceremony. Have you ever seen animals celebrate marriage? They just live together. The wedding ceremony is just part of the culture. For example, in some Confucius or Catholic cultures of the past, where divorce was utterly prohibited, even if the groom died on the night of the wedding ceremony, the bride was still considered widowed and had to live in celibacy for the rest of her life. There were even crazy instances where, if a woman was raped, she had no choice but to marry the rapist. In some countries, I heard that if a man wanted to get married, he had to risk his life and kidnap the bride. If you are born into a particular culture, then that is what you accept as the norm. Marriage is a cultural phenomenon.

If you came to Europe and lived separated from Korean society your views would be drastically different from those of your parents. I heard that in France, half of the couples choose to enter into contracts for marriage relationships. That is a very different culture compared to Korea. Culture can vary according to generation, country, or religion. Because your culture is different from your parents', you cannot avoid conflicting with them when it comes to making a choice. As long as you belong to a different culture and are not willing to accept your parents' values, then naturally, expect conflict. If you do not want the conflict, then choose to accept your parents' old Koreans' ways. But never say "My parents are wrong, foolish, unreasonable, and outdated." They have their views and values. Respect them; don't say that only your values are noble. Parents have their way; you have yours. Respect them and walk your path.

However, listening to you, I cannot help but think that you do not have a thought of your own. You neither follow your parents' ways nor insist upon your own view. It seems your mind is in a contradiction. You want to do what you want but also what your parents want.

What should you do to get married? Open up your repertoire of choice. Tell yourself that anybody who is a guy and who is between twenty and sixty years of age is okay. Open further by allowing divorced men, disabled people, and foreigners to enter your pool. Now, look around. There are so many men that meet this condition! You narrow them down to your own choice; that is why you can't get married. No man in the world is waiting for you, preparing himself to meet your conditions. Men too, are looking for women that meet their conditions. People seek others who can please; they do not seek to please others. If you insist on the conditions that you set out, you will never get married.

Many women do not try to be a good woman for a man, yet they seek a man good for them. Many men are the same. People seek others to be good for them but do not seek to be good for others. If that is the case, even if you do get married, after living a married life for real, you will be let down. You will be disappointed that your guy does not perfectly fit into the dream of the ideal man you had. If you truly, sincerely, desperately want to get married, discard the thought, "Which man will make me happy?"

Walking the narrow alley of Gamla stan, Stockhom

Make up your mind and just think "If it is a guy, all other things don't matter, I'll be grateful to him just for marrying me." If you marry on such a basis, you will only have good things to discover. Marriage will become happier and happier. Nevertheless, if your expectations are too high, even those nice guys do not look satisfactory. Lower your expectations.

Think for yourself. Why do you ask why you should get married? You ask because you want to get married.

I do not want to get married

A young man said, "My values conflict with my duties. I am thirty-two years old. I have two older sisters. Last year, the younger of the sisters finally got married. Now the whole family is expecting me to get married. I feel uncomfortable. I have never thought about getting married. I have no particular desire for marriage or children. I am used to living by myself.

The problem is that my father is the only son and so am I. That means if I do not get married, I cannot pass on my family name [which is regarded important in Korean culture.]. My father has a rock-solid position on marriage. He believes it is my duty. I tried to change my point of view but it would not change. Frankly, I do not want to get married and I don't want children. However, I softened my tone considerably and told my father, 'I think I will get divorced if I marry. I am not sure about this.' My father said, 'It's okay. You may divorce if you really have to. But don't say that you are not going to get married at all.' What should I do?"

First, if you are over twenty, you make your own decisions about your life. You can be a monk or a priest or whatever. Your parents love you. So you take their advice seriously, but you make the call. It is your life, nobody else's. However, do not bluntly say, "I am not getting married. Please stay out of my life." Tell your father, "I understand what you mean. I will get married." When your parents ask you when you are going to get married, just tell them, "I am looking for a girl but haven't found one." Just do it like that. Be smooth. Let me ask you something different, are you not interested in women?

"No. That is not the case."

There are four types of people. Men interested in women. Women interested in men. These two are called heterosexuals. Men interested in men and women interested in women are called homosexuals. Those who have interest in both men and women are called bisexuals. Lastly, there are people interested in neither, the asexuals. This is what research says.

Say an asexual became a monk or a priest. This person might not cause any problem related to sex but that does not mean the person has attained much spirituality. However, if this person got married, that would be disastrous. The wife sexually would want her husband but his body would not react; he is like a piece of wood. She might get him to have sex a few times but eventually she will get hurt. She can suspect him of having an extramarital affair or not loving her. Because on the outside, his body is perfectly normal.

I consult with numerous people and meet lots of different people. There was a man who was homosexual. He suppressed his nature, got married, and had two children. But he could not stand it any longer and came out. It was devastating to his wife and parents. So I told them,

"Everyone has the right to be happy. Your husband has the right to be happy. Does duty come before right? No. You have to accept him as is. You can either give him a divorce and let him go his way or stay with him but approve of his orientation." This mutual understanding and acceptance is what we need. Don't be blinded by distractions.

You said you are none of these cases. But you said you are not interested in marriage. If that is how you feel, that is how you may live. If your family or your duty forces you to get married, you might continue that marriage for a year or two, but eventually, it could break. You were expecting a divorce and your father even endorsed it. However, what about the precious daughter of another family who enters a marriage pre-determined for divorce?

Marriage is about giving up at least half of your rights. You give up yourself and accept the other. If you give up 100 percent, your marriage will be 100 percent successful. If you renounce half, there is a fifty-fifty chance of success. If you want to get married, you want it to be at least 50 percent successful, right? But looking at you, I can see that you are not willing to compromise your values. That means you are not ready for marriage. You make the decision. You are an adult, thirty-two years old.

Korean War Memorial

On the other hand, try to reach a mutual understanding with your parents. Be understanding of your father. "I see that in my father's circumstances, that could be his wish." That does not mean you have to abandon your values. Before you turned twenty, your parents were the greatest supporters you ever had. After twenty, sometimes they can become the greatest obstruction.

When Gautama Siddhartha, the future Buddha, told his father of his resolve to become an ascetic, what was the king's reaction? He was fiercely opposed. Had Gautama listened to his father, would he have become the Buddha? How much pain did Jesus give to his mother? Jesus died at the age of thirty-three. Imagine what it was like for Mary to hold his body in her lap. Just imagine. We say Jesus was great, but what was it like for his parents?

Go your way, walk your path. You are not doing wrong to your parents. If you accept and agree with your parents, then follow. But don't obey when you disagree. Because then, you will end up blaming your parents for any failures or regrets, and you will become enemies with them.

I find it hard to express myself

A man asked, "I find it extremely difficult to express what I feel or think. When I argue, in particular, people point out that I just insist without any logic. I am not good with words. How can I express myself better?"

First, do not try to defeat anyone with your tongue. There is no way you will benefit even if you win. Just say, "You are right" and get over it. Second, you have to understand what exactly is inside you that you want to express. Actually, we do not know entirely what we harbor, thus the saying, "I also do not know myself." You need practice and training to better understand your mind.

There are two ways to become aware of your mind. First is the path of meditation, where deep meditation brings an understanding of your subconscious. Second, you can open up and talk about your deep mind as we do here in Jungto Society through the "Mind Sharing" program. When a participant comes into this Mind Sharing program, for the first two days or so, one will keep talking about one's thoughts and not the mind. But on about the third day, one will start distinguishing between thoughts and mind and start understanding the latter.

About ninety percent of what we say are our thoughts, not our mind. But thoughts and mind are different. Thoughts come from the conscious; the mind is rooted in the subconscious. We say, "You are full of thoughts," but not, "You are full of minds." We say, "My mind hurts," not "My thought hurts." Emotions belong to the mind; reasoning is closer to thoughts. If the behavior is to change, thoughts have to change; but more importantly, the mind has to change. However, because the mind is rooted in the subconscious, it is difficult to change. So first you have to know your state. And then try opening and expressing the mind lightly.

We call this "Mind Sharing" in Jungto Society. Unlike the people in the Western culture, Koreans are taught from youth that it is better to suppress their thoughts and emotions and look calm to others. It is thought more important to remain quiet and polite. But this strategy of suppression has a serious backlash. If you suppress, you will explode. Many Koreans have suppressed energy accumulated in them because the school system and the family culture did not allow them to express themselves freely. So I find it useful to do "Mind Sharing" where one intentionally tries to express their mind. Because we are a community of practitioners, when we finish a Dharma Talk or an event like today's, we always get together to do Mind Sharing.

Express your mind naturally. For example, after listening to my talk today, it is okay to say, "I found it a bit boring." I know you are worried that such an expression might upset me. But if you say, "I found it boring" that is not judging whether I did good or bad. You are merely expressing what you felt. I should not feel bad about those things. Actually, it helps me because I will take that into account for my future talks.

At times, when you speak of your truthful feelings, the other person can get hurt. Then you decide not to speak at all. In both cases, you are being unskillful. You should be able to express your mind lightly, what you felt, and separate that from an act of holding someone accountable. Frankly stating your mind should not be taken as a criticism. It is not to start an argument; it is only to express the emotions. This is not to start a right-or-wrong debate.

As such, you have to keep practicing the methods to bring out your mind. Do not worry about losing the argument. But do care about expressing your mind well. If you are not good at this, you will keep running into misunderstandings, whether it be about a date, love, marriage, or social life. If you can express your deep mind to your loved one who is to live with you for life, that greatly eliminates stress. If you both express frankly and share your mind, there can be some minor quarrels, but on the whole, you will be a happy couple.

On the contrary, there are couples who pride in being well-educated elites, and they say that they never fought once in their life. But in truth, they have never shared their minds; they are strangers, cold to one another. How can you live thinking that expressing yourself somehow hurts your pride? That is one serious ego. You will be uncomfortable because you have things in you that you want to bring out but never do. Your spouse will also be uncomfortable because they can never understand you. Try getting used to expressing yourself although that might cause some minor quarrels. But never blame others. Practice and practice.

Inquisitive

If you realize that all your images are not images,
in other words, if you realize that the things that you say are big or small,
right or wrong, good or bad are actually neither big nor small,
neither right nor wrong, good nor bad then you are enlightened.

I want to know more about the Diamond Sutra.

/

Indianapolis

/

An elderly man asked, "I have lived in Indianapolis for forty-two years. I am a Catholic turning seventy next year. For the past thirty years, I studied Buddhist canons by myself whenever I had time. Can you please explain to me the meaning of the following stanza in the Diamond Sutra?

All images are empty
If you see that all images are not images
You will see the Buddha."

Can you tell me how you understood it?

"I think it means that when you realize that what you are being greedy about does not actually exist, I mean, that it is impermanent, you can let go better. You can live more for others. I thought that a better understanding of this stanza could be the key to understanding Buddhism."

Did such understanding change your life?

"I think it did. Quite significantly."

Do you see these baskets in the front? Is the yellow basket larger or smaller than the white one?

"It is larger."

Is the yellow basket larger or smaller than this container with sand?

"It is smaller."

The yellow basket was the same object, but you once said that it is larger and once smaller. Then let's just think of this basket alone. Is it large or small?

"It is about medium."

No. When we say something is large, small, or middle-sized, we are comparing it to something, some image in our head. That comparison makes possible the language of large or small. We call this "relative." In other words, the basket is larger or smaller or medium, relative to another image. When you said it is large, you compared it with a smaller image.

When you said it is small, you compared it with a larger image. You can see that a perception is relative.

"Yes. I understand."

Then if we part with such a relative view, in an absolute sense, what can we say of this basket?

"It does not exist."

What do you mean it does not exist? It is right before your eyes. Do not give conceptual answers. The answer to my question, "Is it large or small?" would be, "It is neither large nor small."

All images are empty

If you see that all images are not images

You will see the Buddha.

All images are empty means that, "All images or notions that I have fabricated are empty." Here, "image" means something that we endow and believe has a substance, such as the qualities of large, small, right, wrong, and so forth. Empty is different from nihilism. Empty is only to describe that something is without substance, not the true image, not actual, not real, but only a delusion.

If you see that all images are not images, you will see the Tathágata. This means that if you realize all your images are not images, in other words, if you realize that the things that you say are big or small, right or wrong, good or bad are actually neither big nor small, neither right nor wrong, neither good nor bad then you will see the Buddha, then you will reach Buddhahood, then that is enlightenment.

This is a cup. But there are cups for water, milk, coffee, wine, whiskey, and many more. If we are confined by the name we give to the cup, a coffee cup should always be used for drinking coffee, a water cup for water, a milk cup for milk. Say someone came to you and asked you for a cup of coffee and you say, "Oh, I am sorry, we don't have any coffee cups." This is mistaking an image for something real. This "thing" that exists can be used for drinking coffee or water or whatever. If undefined, it can hold anything. If you release your fixed ideas, it can be anything. A coffee cup is not only for coffee. If it holds water, it becomes a water cup. Pour milk into it, it becomes a milk cup. You can even put rice in it, and it becomes a rice bowl. Put in soup, and it's a soup bowl. If your baby needs to urgently urinate in a restaurant, it can even become a toilet. Do you see how free you become? This is the message. This is an explanation of Buddhism's essential philosophy of "emptiness" without using the word "empty."

However, just as being attached to an image is an error, being attached to the emptiness of an image is another error. You can think of it this way. You already have cups for drinking water, coffee, and beer. You have cups specified for those purposes. But insisting that "all notions are empty," and using just one cup for drinking water and beer and even eating rice, is an

error. Emptiness has become un-empty, an image, instead of freeing you from images. So, in your daily life, just use a water cup for water, a coffee cup for coffee. Other cups have other uses. But do not be restricted to the name of the cup. If you don't have a particular cup, don't hesitate to substitute it with another.

Say someone asks you, "In which direction does Korea lie?" You cannot answer that. It cannot be answered if you do not have a relative position. A Chinese will say Korea lies to the east. A Japanese would say Korea is to the west. Russians will say it is to the south. There are roads to Korea, but their directions are different depending on where they start. The direction is not fixed; it changes according to where you are, but still, there does exist a direction that leads you to the destination.

In Buddhism, we refer to this as, "The Dharma (or teaching or path) is not fixed." "Empty" does not mean that there is nothing; the meaning is beyond there being nothing or something. When you realize that all things(dharmas) are empty, it means that the direction that person should be headed can be either east or west, north or south according to the condition of the person. But again, this given direction should not be fixed. Attaching to language is an error. However, if you believe that there is no such thing as a correct direction or you should not choose any direction, you have learned the wrong lesson. This creates an image of emptiness. Emptiness is supposed to free you from images, not create one. You see, saying "You cannot say there is one direction," means the same as "You can say that all directions can work." However, the direction that works arises out of the conditions.

Making an image is called a form (rūpa) and not making an image is called emptiness (śūnyatā). In the Heart Sutra is a famous saying, "Form is emptiness. Emptiness is form." Why does the sentence repeat? Why not just say, "Form is emptiness"? What does "Emptiness is form" imply? It repeats in order to emphasize that the two are the same. It explains that the phenomenon and essence co-exist. If you say the phenomenon is unreal and only the essence is real, you are only half-right. It is like saying, "This cup is neither large nor small." This view in the essence-perspective is only half-right. If asked under a specific circumstance, for example, compared with a smaller cup, you should be able to answer in a phenomenon-perspective and say, "It is large." This is rūpa, the world of form. You are able to say it is large or small according to particular conditions. This is dependent arising (Pratītyasamutpāda).

But on the other hand, if the cup is taken out of its conditions, its context, then you should be able to say that "It is neither big nor small. It is only what it is. It is empty." Do you see how this teaching liberates us? Do you think Zen masters live beyond ethics and morals? No. They would normally comply with the social norms but when ethics start to oppress the people, they have the insight to liberate people from them. The focus is on whether people are living freely and happily, not whether certain morals are being upheld. Ethics exist for the people, not the other way around. The Buddha and Jesus have said the same thing. Their focus was to liberate and empower people. There are many paths people can take to achieve that. The paths are there for humans, not vice versa. The problem is that some institutions put their teachings before the people and try to mold humans into their dogma.

What is practice?

Ann Arbor

A gentleman asked, "I am a professor. I received neither a tenure nor a doctoral degree. I have lots of work preparing for lectures and writing my dissertation at the same time. My mind is diffused and distracted. I read in a Jungto Society leaflet that you promote 100-day, 1,000-day, and 10,000-day practices. What is a practice? I want to be awake to this moment and feel the things happening here and now. I wish my mind was not so noisy. But I frequently find my mind continuing to grasp. How can I let go? How do I do practice?"

You cannot do everything you want. You have to make a choice. There are choices about whether or not to do something. There are choices in what to do between A and B. It is a matter of priority. What is your number one priority? Do not say all your issues bear the same weight. There must be a priority. Which is foremost?

"It is my Ph.D."

Then leave it as number one. What is number two?

"My lecture. There is a conflict between the Ph.D. and lecturing. Tenure is important for me but not as important as my Ph.D. I can get a tenure from other schools."

Then how will you make your living?

"You have rightly pointed out. That is precisely the problem I face."

On what earnings do you make your living presently?

"I get paid working as a professor."

Then making a living should be number one. You must live first to do anything else.

"Why is that?"

You must eat and live first. Only then can you do other things. So economy comes first. Do you have a family?

"Yes. Actually, my family is more important than the two I mentioned. I omitted my family to make my question simple. To keep my job, I need to

finish my dissertation in a year. That means it is due in August of next year. So my dissertation is more important."

Your Ph.D. is directly linked to making a living. First you should discuss this with your wife. Ask her if it is okay to concentrate on the dissertation for a year. Or borrow some money to sustain yourself for a year. Your living must be secure first. Your wife could work or you could borrow some money. Solve that problem first. Then do your studies.

"I believe my job and my degree are compatible. My dissertation is almost finished. My problem is that when I do something, I cannot wholly concentrate. When I try to do one thing, I am still thinking of other things. I understand that Zen practice can make you awake at this present moment. That is why I came to this Dharma Talk today. I am learning more about practice, but I still don't understand what it is. I don't believe that a 100-day practice can cure my problem. What I really want to know is what it means to practice. If you practice, can you be clear about your purpose, mind happy and light, able to act without being seized with other thoughts?"

There exist such practice methods. But that is not the ultimate solution. Say there is a 2-meter (6.6 feet) high wall in front of you. You try to jump over it but cannot. You tried ten times but always failed. Then someone at your back points a gun at you and threatens that if you do not jump

over it, you will be shot. You hear gunfire. You will surely jump over it. You think and say that your Ph.D. is important but you cannot concentrate. That means your conscious mind thinks, "I have to do it," but your subconscious thinks, "I can still manage even if I don't get it done." That is why distracted thoughts keep arising. If you really feel an urgency, if you really feel that if you don't get it done in a year, you will lose your job, then you can't do anything but concentrate. You will hold a book even in the washroom. You will read in between your lectures. You will cut down sleep and study while eating. Focus is done naturally. That you are distracted means that you feel a pressure but still your subconscious is not agreeing to the urgency. What does that mean? You have nothing to worry about. You will make a living without it. Listen to the whisper from your subconscious.

Re-check whether that is really important for you. Do this, do that, if you can do everything, that would be ideal. But it is not possible to do everything. Number your issues and concentrate. If you have trouble concentrating, then realize that what you pursue is not urgent. Then discard it.

"Can I discard one of them?"

Which one? You cannot throw out your family. Actually that is why you can focus more on your studies. Family is not an obstacle. You contradict yourself; you want to make less effort but still get a Ph.D.

"Are you telling me to try harder?"

Trying means you are doing something you do not want to do. Nobody tries to do something they like. They just do it. Do kids try to play more games? No. They just play. They play whatever the cost or restriction. Trying is a word you use when you do something by forcing yourself because you are doing something you dislike. If you don't like something, don't do it. Never try to do something.

"I seem to dislike what I am doing but I have to finish it. I don't know."

There is no such thing. Don't do it if you don't want to. If doing what you do not want gives you profit, then you have to persevere. You might hate what you are doing, but you are doing it for a gain. You have to do what you dislike.

Having a Ph.D. means you did research in your field and produced an original view of your own. Creating something is best done when you are engaged in an activity you love. Nobody should be able to stop you from doing it. However, you are studying not because you like it but you need a Ph.D. for your job.

There are many students here. When they say studying is difficult, it means they are doing something against their liking. For instance, they study because they know they will get a better job if they complete their studies. That is why the whole process is so arduous and difficult. If you think, "I don't care about the job, I will study what I like," then studying is like playing. If you don't want to do it, then don't do it. You have this greed in you. Do you think you can practice Zen with that greed? Can you pray earnestly? Meditation is not a formality. It is about observing the contradiction that you harbor. Then you solve the conflict. If the conflict is damaging you, you have to discard it even though you want to continue. That is why the teaching tells you to let go.

"I will think about what you said. Thank you. It helped me. I had never thought about this in the way you explained."

Why do I have to do 108 prostrations?

Newport News

A middle-aged woman asked, "You always tell us to do 108 prostrations. Why do we have to do that? I want to know why I have to bow, apart from doing it as an exercise."

Let's say two people are lying down. They start an argument. Then they sit up. They continue to fight. Then they stand up. The conflict gets intense. Then they stick up their heads. Look at their physical posture. They are erect, shoulders are tight, heads up, eyes wide open and intense, and voices are big. This physical shape is typical of a person who believes that they are right. That is how our body expresses that mental state.

When you believe you are right and the other person is wrong, your anger reaches its peak. When you start realizing that you are not quite right after all, your eye starts to look down, your head lowers. You say, "I am sorry," and lower your upper body. That is bowing. If you feel that you have done wrong, you kneel. If you feel even more guilty, you put your forehead to the ground. That is how the body expresses your mind.

Kneeling and putting the forehead on the ground is the bodily expression of the mind that has renounced the "I am right" attitude. Prostration expresses, "I have nothing to claim that I am right. I have done wrong, I repent."

There are three benefits of prostration. First, it is an excellent overall physical exercise. It is better than any other exercise. Let's say you have 15 minutes to exercise. I tell you that bowing is the best.

Second, other exercises are only physical, but prostration has a psychological effect. It releases you from the toxic thought, "I am right." This relieves you of stress. Stress arises when you stick with the idea, "I am right." There is no stress when you say, "I am wrong." People in modern society are often poisoned by this self-righteous perception. This seriously stresses them. Bowing will help.

Third, using auto-suggestive writing will help further. A writing that is intended to influence your subconscious is called a prayer. Many people like to pray to ask for help. "Oh, great Buddha, make my mind peaceful." This is asking for help. This is not how you should pray. When you pray, keep suggesting to yourself, "My mind is at peace. Thank you, Buddha." If you repeat this prayer every time you bow, you can tell yourself 108 times. If you have a conflict with your husband, tell yourself, "He is right. I need wisdom." You will be surprised to find how you habitually think, "You are wrong. What do you know?" when you confront different views. If you do this auto-suggestion, you will be calm and neutral when your husband tells you something. This is why you do prostration.

Then why the number 108? It does not matter whether you do 100 or 103. It is just that in the Buddhist tradition, we say that there are 108 defilements. So the number 108 is a symbol of cleansing yourself of the 108 sufferings. You bow not to please the Buddha but to repent of your ignorance. This is purely to look into yourself and understand your ignorance. Such an idea does not conflict with any religion. But if you are a Christian or have another faith and are not comfortable, for example, do 103 prostrations. There were 103 Catholic martyrs in Korea at the end of the Joseon dynasty when the kingdom oppressed the Western religion. So the number 103 can be used to symbolize remembering them. You see, the number itself is irrelevant.

Bowing repeatedly is not easy. You will have many thoughts as you go on. At first, you might feel sorry for your husband, but then, on second thought, anger might arise. "It is definitely the case that my husband was wrong and not me!" Then as you continue, a mind of repentance might come back. Your mind will continue to fluctuate. However, in the entire process, you will slowly work toward melting your ego. You start to understand your spouse or your partner. Understanding them means becoming free from the stress that came from not understanding them.

When you feel, "I cannot understand that guy!" you get angrier, your voice gets louder, and the mind is perplexed. This lack of understanding, this ignorance is the source of stress. Once you understand why that guy or girl was like that, your stress goes away. So I say, "Do not try to be understood but try to understand." It is because you desire to be understood that

you get stressed. If you do the understanding, your stress will go away. That is why you bow. It is arduous, you sweat, you want to quit, but you continue. The will to continue is the will to change your personality, to conquer your karma. Without a strong will power, you cannot bow 108 times. Repeated bowing is psychologically helpful to people regardless of their religion.

Let me sum it up. First, it is good for your physical health. Second, it helps soften your ego. Third, using a prayer brings a change to your subconscious. This remarkably reduces your stress.

Does it help advance world peace if I meditate?

Princeton University

A student asked, "I understand that you practice meditation and engage in peace movement socially at the same time. What does meditation have to do with bringing forth world peace? How do you see the relation between the two? What can we do to promote peace through meditation?"

Normally, if you have anger in you, you hate other things. Your action becomes violent and destructive. Advancing peace with hatred in your heart is impossible. Your mind has to be peaceful first. If you criticize social issues while at peace, that wisdom helps solve the issue.

The key to meditation is having peace of mind. There are three conditions to meditation. First, your mind should be relaxed and without any tension. Second, your mind should be focused on one thing. It can be your breath, sensation or whatever. Third, as you focus, you must be awake and maintain the state of mindfulness.

When you do breathing meditation, for example, you must fully relax

Princeton University

your body and mind first. Then your mind focuses on the tip of the nose. It becomes thoroughly mindful of the breathing. We breathe every moment, however, never notice. Use some focus, and you can notice that you are breathing.

When breath comes in, notice, "breath is coming in." When it goes out, notice, "breath is going out." If you are breathing fast, notice, "breath is fast." If your breathing is soft, notice, "breath is soft." It is not the technique of breathing; you are not breathing in any particular way. You only notice breathing as it happens naturally.

This is not as easy as it sounds. You keep thinking of things that happened in the past, or things to do in the future. Your mind soon wanders off, and you lose awareness of your breathing.

Do not be attached to the past or to the future. The past is gone; the future is not yet here. Focus only on the here and now. Focus on your breath; notice your breath. Your mind will become more relaxed and your breath more subtle. When breath becomes subtle, it is easier to lose awareness of it because more thoughts arise. So you have to focus more. Keep going like this, and then your breath will become very, very soft. You will even notice the difference in air temperature when it goes in and out, and even the sensation of the tiny hairs swaying in your nostrils.

You can become fully and clearly mindful of the subtlest of sensations. As a result, your mind reaches peace. At this point, you are ready to engage in activities to promote peace. If you harbor anger in your heart yet try to promote peace, you are likely to end up fighting in the name of peace.

How to bring about political change

A man asked, "I am frustrated, angry, and uneasy. I firmly believe that we need a fundamental political change. I am concerned about unfairness, climate change, corruption, degradation of democracy, and many others. What do you think is the Buddhist method to effectively bring about a political change? For example, what do you think about peaceful demonstration or civil disobedience?"

What is a Buddhist method? Buddhist method means being most effective in the given situation. The essence of Buddhist teachings is the Middle Way. The Middle Way means "the best in the given conditions." The Middle Way is not fixed. When the conditions change, the Middle Way also changes. It is the best only in the given particular time and space. It is always the condition of the conditions that is critical.

Our thoughts are based on our conscious so they can change quickly. But our emotions are based on the subconscious so they don't change easily. In Buddhism, we call this karma. They are habits ingrained in us. They

Ven. PomnyunSunim is one of the few monks
that can explain the wisdom of Buddhism in the simplest and clearest words.
—Professor Hebbar, George Washington University

take a long time to change. You cannot change them overnight. When you feel frustrated because you don't change easily, you might start to hate yourself, thinking, "I am a total failure." This is self-torture. This can be directed at others. Meaning, when other people do not change, you become angry at them. But you see, this karma is extremely difficult to change. Numerous mistakes and practices need to be made. It takes time. To accelerate the change, you need to give a strong impetus to the subconscious. Your restlessness, your hastiness, the desire to change or change quickly – these are what create anger, hatred, and despair. We need to understand this. That is where we begin.

Society is the same. That is the reason why we study history. Individual historical events are full of failures. But in the long run, through the long-term perspective of history, all events gather to create a success. If you try something impossible, you will fail in the first few trials. But accumulate the attempts and failure; then you will gradually make progress. So in the long run, history is a success story.

For example, the environmental crisis that we have created is truly life-threatening. But changing the environmentally-not-so-friendly lifestyle is not easy. How we live is an already-formed habit. This toxic perception that the more you consume, the better off you are has become pervasive. Increased consumption is destroying the planet but people continue to live like that. No matter how hard environmentalists try, this desperate situation might not improve a bit. Then does this mean we have nothing to do but despair? No. We might not be able to reverse the tide and heal the earth. However, our efforts might delay the onset of the doomsday. Also, when an environmental crisis breaks out, if we have made collective efforts, we might be able to find a solution faster.

If what we do is right, we need to continue doing it. Give it your best. If you can speed up the process, that is good. But this needs some research. There might be a way to speed up a positive outcome in a particular situation, but there is no one-thing-fits-all kind of general solution. It is the same for politics. If you try to change things quickly, you end up being frustrated and angry; this can increase your tendency to resort to violence. Look far and proceed steadily. Only then can you sustain your efforts. Only when our efforts are sustained, do we have a higher chance of change.

How should I understand religion?

A man explained, "I am traveling right now. How should I understand religious wars? I have experienced three religions on my trip. In Korea and China, I met those who practiced Buddhism. In Iran and Turkey, I met those who practiced Islam. In Western Europe, I met those who practiced Catholicism. Religion sometimes seems to help humanity greatly, but again at times it really seems to degrade some people. There were wars in the name of religion. How should I view religion?"

There are two types of religions. One is a primitive religion that evolved naturally. Another is a more advanced – higher religion. Primitive religions always base their thinking on reward-or-punishment approach. Do something good and you will be rewarded. Do something bad and you will be punished. It is a tit-for-tat logic. Many religions base their doctrine on this idea. This ancient thought has solidified into law in the Code of Hammurabi. The tit-for-tat idea is common in all primitive religions.

But when it comes to Jesus or the Buddha, religion takes on a different color. It is no longer a simple tit-for-tat, reward for good, revenge for bad.

In primitive religions, the people who crucified Jesus should have fallen into burning hell. But what did Jesus say? "Forgive them, for they know not what they do." This is the God of forgiveness, God of love.

If you seek secular or material success through religion, and believe in the religion for that reason, then that religion to you is a primitive religion. It does not matter what the name of the religion is.

If you see religions fighting against each other, it is safe to say that the fighting has nothing to do with the original teachings of the founders – Jesus, Buddha, Mohammed, etc. These religious fighters are pursuing secular profits under the name of religion. What deepens a religious conflict is that you believe you and only you are right. Anybody can make a mistake or be wrong, but if you ask some religious leaders, they say they know the "Truth." So people of different religions, or even those in the same religion with different views, find it hard to harmonize and cooperate with one another. However, I believe as the society becomes more pluralistic toward religion, this will get better.

The essence of the teachings of Jesus or the Buddha lies not in their "world of dogma" but actually in the real human world. If you look at it, our society has evolved such that now, legally speaking, gender, racial and national equality have been achieved. Even sexual orientations are starting to be respected. Physical disabilities cannot be a reason for discrimination. But look at how religions react. They tell a suffering person that they suffer because they have sinned or have bad karma. They are effectively telling

Last talk in Europe
— Trinity College Dublin

you that disability is a sin, being born a woman is a disadvantage, having an uncommon sexual orientation is depravity.

Religious wars have nothing to do with Jesus or the Buddha. They have everything to do with the people who seek material profit disguised as religion.

Why would a religion ever need huge shrines, churches, stupas, monasteries, and temples? Who has built them? Kings and emperors. When Christianity was recognized in Rome, the emperor became the head of the church. What better symbolism to witness the secularization of religion? Do not mistake these secular agendas as religion. However, since so many modern religions have become secular and corrupt, therein lies the delusion of religion. But again, I stress that this does not mean that Jesus's teachings have lost meaning or that the teachings themselves are corrupt.

We have to open our eyes to these phenomena. What we think as a war of religions is nothing but a war of profit, material gains or ideological competitions. Religion is being abused. Too often, heavenly teachings have become a tool for pursuing worldly gains.

How can I be a good counsellor?

Tampa

A man asked, "I work as a doctor. By nature of my profession, I do a lot of counselling. I meet many patients with depression, stress, particularly those who want to commit suicide. I am an ethnic Korean but my patients are mostly American. I feel I need some special approach in my consultation. Patients have come through other doctors, so I think I should use some new technique for better effect. I did some research myself into this too. How can I be good at counselling?"

In my experience, the most important thing in counselling is that you fully admit, "I cannot change another person." The thought that "I can change someone" is extremely dangerous. If you start on that premise, when you fail, you will hate yourself and be stressed. However, a human fundamentally cannot help another person. I mean, one can help by giving food or fixing a broken bone, for example, but one cannot change another person's character or habit or thought. This mental sphere is unstirred by foreign intervention.

Then why is it that so many people say they have changed after listening to my talks? They come to me and admit that they changed, that I helped them. Let's be precise. It is true that they found the Talks helpful. But I never gave them help. They were helped because they decided to receive the teachings; they helped themselves.

There are two causes of depression. First is mental trauma. Second is a disruption in the body's endocrinal system. Depression has yet to be fully explained by science. Lighter cases are cured. But serious cases mostly seem to end up in the tragic event of a suicide. When a patient comes in, take it lightly. If you take it too seriously, with a sense of conviction or obligation to change another person, that you will give help, that is dangerous. You can, in reverse, be infected by the disease. If you don't try to give help, you won't be diseased. Just listen to them light-heartedly.

The attitude with which you perform counselling is extremely important. First is listening. Second is agreeing. You say, "Yes. I agree. Yes. That can be so." Third is relating your real-life experiences. Not something from the books but something from your personal experience. "I had this experience one time, and I overcame it by such and such." Do not tell them to do as you did; that could be offensive. Just say in this way, "I heard a monk's Dharma Talk once and it helped me a great deal."

There is one very big difference between a doctor and myself. I am not paid. This has so much to do with the actual outcome of therapy. If you are paid, you are dealing with a customer. You cannot make a customer upset. You have a certain responsibility. You cannot give the wrong treatment.

All of these practices make you consider many things. In many cases, you end up not being able to give straight talks. A straight talk might hurt your customer, or make the customer uncomfortable or angry. But I am not paid. I do not claim I am a professional in this field. I am free to give as straight and direct a talk as I want. It is not without trouble, but because I receive no money, people do not make a controversy out of it. But if doctors follow my method, they can't run a business.

Some might say that my method is more effective, but that is not necessarily so. My service is free, so if ten people come and even if only one benefits, the remaining nine people have no reason to complain about that. That one successful person, on the other hand, will go around and talk about how great it was. This is advertisement effect. Hospital is the opposite. Out of ten people, if nine were healed, they would remain silent because they paid for it anyway. But the one case that was a failure will continue to denounce or even sue the doctor. So the money they make counterbalances the fame they lose. For me, the money I do not receive instead enhances my reputation. You can see that there are many factors at play.

The most important point, I stress, is that you do not try to cure another person. But a doctor has the responsibility to cure people. Herein lies the dilemma. However, you have to put down that thought if you don't want to be stressed.

Lighten your heart. "My knowledge, my skill in medicine is limited. This is better than nothing when curing a person, but still, it is a meager knowledge. I just do my best." With this kind of attitude, you are able to be thankful for all things, live happily as a doctor, and not be stressed over treating a new patient. If you keep being attached to the thought that you must cure someone, you will be stressed. You will make money but you will be tired. Even if you meet healthy people, if you meet them for a whole day, that is tiring. You are meeting sick people all day long. It brings you money, but how stressful is that?

Learn to love yourself first. A patient's life is important but you should know yours is more precious. Protect yourself. Only then can you help the patients and help heal the world.

"My talent is small. I cannot give an enormous help to that person. But I can be a good listener." Make that the starting point. You go from there. Lower your expectations. Then when you cure someone, it will be fun. You will be excited to do new research. If you are bound by the thought, "I must cure this person," then you will remain in your own thoughts. Then you cannot be a good listener. Listen to someone with your heart. "Why does that person want to die?" Study carefully about what results your consultation produces. Analyze and do research. This kind of talk was very helpful, that kind was even more helpful, and so forth. You can also produce your own statistics. Keep doing this and then the more patients you meet, the more experienced you become, the greater an expert you become – instead of being stressed out. I think this kind of perspective would be useful.

How can I gain merits as a doctor?

Houston

A man asked, "I am an Oriental medicine doctor. I met a respected monk twelve years ago who told me that I have a good job so I should generate a lot of merits [Buddhist term meaning actions that bring good results, good karma]. But I have too many patients now and my body is so tired that I cannot fully commit to consultations. I feel my treatments are not working as well and I feel bad but I really cannot do my best when I am so fatigued. Then I get worried because I thought I might be losing the merits that I gained. This troubles me. Is it better for me to rest when I feel tired or should I keep tending to the patients despite my fatigue? Which is better for my merits?"

Damaging or harming others is a bad thing. If I do not help others that is neither good nor bad. Helping others is deemed good. But doing good is not an obligation. It is a choice.

However, attacking, beating or killing others, taking or stealing other people's property, sexually harassing or assaulting others are things that are prohibited. There is an obligation not to do these things. Lying or harming others is also prohibited.

However, helping others is a matter of choice. Caring for your infants is an obligation, but caring for your old parents is a choice. If you care for the elderly, that is good, but even if you don't, it's not evil. If you do not care for your baby, that is evil, but caring for them does not make you good. You are only doing what you are supposed to do.

When making choices in your life, first and foremost, you should be happy. If you are in pain and you want to help others, you might be able to do it for a short while, but very soon you will quit. Suppressing your needs, yielding to others, persevering against your willpower – these things you will rarely withstand more than three times. There will come a time when you explode.

If you benefit at the expense of others, that is also not long lasting. Because the person being sacrificed will not remain still. Other people benefiting while you suffer is also not sustainable. You will not be idle and let it be that way. People say if you help others despite your pains, that is a great good. Indeed, it is rare. But in terms of practice, that is not the right way. Society might praise such a person, but that person is not a good practitioner. Because such an act is short-lived and self-consuming.

Everyone who sacrifice themselves will want compensation. They cling to the notion "I made a sacrifice" so they want other people to recognize or reward them. If their wish is not met, they become dissatisfied. It is the same with couples. A wife might have sacrificed herself for her husband's career or to raise the children. If her sacrifice is not properly compensated or acknowledged by her husband or children, she will develop anger or a grudge. Wife and husband start to fight, mother and children become enemies. This is not the path of a practitioner.

Therefore, you yourself must be happy first. Do that first. And THEN, if you can make others happy, do it. If you cannot, do not. In that case, not doing it is not evil. The best outcome would be you and others both being happy. That is the true path.

This is why as a doctor, you should be happy first before you try to heal others. You must live before you try to make others live. You must be happy before you try to make others happy. That is the most important. If you have in your mind the tiniest thought that you "helped" someone, you will forever want something in return. That is not the way of a Buddhist practitioner, a Bodhisattva. If you miss this point, whatever you do, karma will follow. Karma can either be good or bad; the point is that it keeps arising. That is why, to the question, "How should I overcome my mind?" the Diamond Sutra teaches us, "Save all sentient beings. But if you have a thought that you saved them, you are no longer a Bodhisattva." The path to liberalization is different from secular paths, paths of good or bad.

Again, I stress that you must be happy first. If parents are unhappy and full of thoughts that they are sacrificing their lives for their children, that is not good for their children. If raising kids was such a pain to the parents, that already makes the children bad. How can such people grow up to be good adults? When you raise kids, you must be happy. You must raise them happily. Your body might be tired but your mind should be joyful. Think like this: "Whatever the case, having a child is much better in my life than not having one."

Listen carefully. The child is a good person only when the parents are happy. Why is this so? Because the child makes others happy. That is a good person. Remember that if the mother is happy raising her child, the child will become a good person. If the mother is grudging, the child will become her enemy. A great many of you are disappointed at your children after they grow up. Parents and children become enemies. In many instances, that is because you have sacrificed against your happiness. Your own happiness is most important.

Think of this. There is a paradox about a doctor's job. If many patients come to visit, it means the doctor is making lots of money. If nobody comes, the doctor will go broke. But is it a better world with fewer patients or more patients? Fewer patients means that the doctor is likely to think, "Why isn't anyone sick these days? They should be sick." This is quite immoral. How can a doctor wish people to be sick? Why does this problem occur? It is because of money. The doctor is thinking in terms of money. If the doctors have fewer patients, then they should actually be happy – they can meditate or volunteer in their free time. Fewer sick people means the suffering in the world has decreased. If fewer people ask me questions, that also means the world is getting better.

The presence of sick people itself is a blessing to the doctor. The doctor can use their skill for the good of the world. If you have a lot of patients, work happily. You might want to sacrifice your eating time or sleeping time for work, but you would do it happily. If you do not do it happily, it is not sustainable. You do not want to lose your health from overworking. A wise person would properly control and balance these factors. Do not be carried away by your emotions. Do not let them destroy your health.

I am also NOT saying that when you've made money, you should care only about your pleasures. If you start enjoying golf or travels more than you enjoy helping the patients, that is not right either. Your relaxation should be to maintain your health. Your primary source of happiness should come from helping your patients.

Be happy that you are giving the patients happiness. Do not think, "I am accumulating merits by helping them." You should be happy purely because you can help them. Only then can you be free. You will be free whether your patient is cured or not, whether patients come to you or not.

Do not be confident of your ability to cure people. In that case, failure can torment you. You see, there is not much that one human can do to help another. Just think to yourself, "I have little knowledge and tiny skill in medicine. I will do my best. If the results are good, that is good, the Buddha has helped. If not, my skill is not good enough." Keep this attitude if you want to be comfortable when dealing with patients. The thought, "I must heal this patient," can produce problems.

The doctor replied, "Thank you for the advice. At least, I am not committing social evils as you have described. I will not abandon the patients but I will take care of my happiness. I will work hard to help others."

Take out that "hard" part. Just say, "I will do what I can to help others." Do so comfortably, with contentment, but not too hard.

"Thank you."